Superactually:

Micro-Essays on
Post-Ironic Life

Superactually:

Micro-Essays on
Post-Ironic Life

Chuk Moran

Winchester, UK
Washington, USA

First published by Zero Books, 2012
Zero Books is an imprint of John Hunt Publishing Ltd., Laurel House, Station Approach,
Alresford, Hants, SO24 9JH, UK
office1@jhpbooks.net
www.johnhuntpublishing.com
www.zero-books.net

For distributor details and how to order please visit the 'Ordering' section on our website.

Text copyright: Chuk Moran 2012

ISBN: 978 1 78099 465 9

A CIP catalogue record for this book is available from the British Library.

Design: Stuart Davies

Printed and bound by CPI Group (UK) Ltd, Croydon, CR0 4YY

We operate a distinctive and ethical publishing philosophy in all
areas of our business, from our global network of authors to
production and worldwide distribution.

CONTENTS

Introduction

Distraction and recurrence give inclinations.

This is a book of very short essays on many topics organized into sections. It is theoretical because it tries to get all the words right. It is radical because it starts from what is accepted among far-out intellectuals and departs in another direction for a different journey. It is contemporary because the topics are.

You should read it because you should read parts of it. First what pops out. Some essays are about things you already care about. Read them. Then read other essays that don't sound interesting, because what you have read will make what you do read more interesting. At the same time, what you read later will make what you read earlier make more sense.

Reading should not always be easy. Sometimes the words of an essay wrap with the warp of the bends sentences need to resemble the ideas they are to express. Read slowly sometimes and review. It is better, here, to understand one thing well than many only poorly. There are many loose ends.

Frequent small examples can make concepts familiar faster. The production of examples is the greatest gift of a good theory. But examples, like inept advocates, can also show just how wrong the argument is that they were supposed to support.

An argument, in itself, is almost always a small thing. It is the explanations, definitions, evidence, contextualization, encouragement, clarification, and listing of subordinate categories that takes time. Arguments alone, without all this support, are easier to disagree with.

The most important power of arguments as conceptual arrangements is that, sometimes, we somehow do not deny them. That they are tempting does not mean that they are strong or for the best. It means that they are worth expressing because they can, and to some extent should, be refused. Qualms fuel thought.

Now, turn to a random page and begin.

Section on Talking

When mammals live together, they purr and bark. Talking gets dinner ready, people to places on time, and merchandise out the door. There are many forces changing the world. Talk is one.

How Are You

When someone says, 'words don't mean, they function,' isn't it a performative contradiction? Doesn't that sentence depend on words meaning? It could, or it could also not. Consider a case where words function rather than mean and, yet, also may still function by meaning.

How are you? 'Fine' means things aren't quite right. 'Good' means we don't have to talk about it. 'Great' means there's some story or good news. 'Not so good' means we're compelled to talk about it. Attacking the question is too mean, because everyone knows the question is not a literal one.

Literalism has almost nothing to do with it. What does the question literally mean? In what manner are you? For what reason, with what meaning, to what effect, by what name or title, to what degree, in what condition, at what price are you (feeling today)? It would be dumb cynicism to accuse the question of lacking literalism. 'How are you?' really means, 'this is your first chance to indicate to me that your disposition should be recog-

4

nized to influence our interaction,' and, 'I'm transitioning politely from greeting to conversation.' It is not an information request as to your present state, we are not really going to discuss your mood now. Instead, if you're in no condition for what is about to happen, let me know now. Otherwise just say 'good.'

We all understand how to work the system, though I doubt we're all conscious of the situation as a language game, or of the words' specialized meaning within the context. How do you resolve this? Do the words mean or function? Do the words mean something, which is so specialized it hardly resembles their definitions in any dictionaries? Or, do the words function in social situations, in a way we need not understand in terms of signification or meaning? And, if the words do signify in this case, their actual meanings still remain unsaid.

Importance

What is important? What is most important?

The underlying question that these queries demand we not ask has received very little attention: what makes things important? It seems that one must have an opinion on what is important, or be beholden to what others say is important. Either way, it is in the service of important things that we will be obliged to act and orient our thinking.

I understand what it means to say something is yellow or unpleasant; what does it mean to say something is important? What is importance? What is most of importance? A commitment that we should attend to a problematic. But this is too inexact because it is too neat. It uses other words rather too easily. That something is important is not the same as saying you should do something about it. Important dates in history. Things that are important do not have normative or ethical force. They are seductive, but not *because* they are seductive or irresistible.

If you think a problem (e.g. illiteracy) is important, it attracts your attention, justifies action, motivates your efforts, and trumps other concerns. You name it as the determinant of consequences and influence, as something with a high social standing, as something everyone ought to be concerned with.

If you say something is important, you encourage others to regard it as important. Importance functions as an imperative on others.

Buzzwords

They are words that buzz, rattle, loose their meaning, inspire connections based only on the presence of this word, again and again: affect.

The buzzword infests utterances, texts, keyword lists: postcolonial. Why not? It sounds hip, it sounds right, I don't want to get cut out because I'm not up to date: best practices.

The word inflects the formation of arguments, provides orientation towards as well as away from: postmodern. It's not certain yet whether the word is or is not appropriate, when its buzz is still fresh, two texts can even apply the word in opposite ways to advantage: mobility.

There is, so far, nothing to lose in using it, no real claim it can be identified with that someone will come along and prove wrong: memory. The word would need a more certain meaning, it is not yet in a state to be opposed: the cloud.

It turns out to describe surprisingly well what has come before, because its uneven universalization is a journey and because it is what we find interesting in our interpretation of most anything: client-oriented. The word doesn't name something altogether new, it just has a more clear vision of what the thing is that we are naming: deliverables.

By its connective tissue, everything appears related, tagged the same, commensurable, related to the particular concerns of each in a community: temporality. All scholars turned out to have been studying meaning, whether they knew it or not. Business was always about optimization, monetization, and the low hanging fruit.

Sometimes the word is more specific, it comes from somewhere and bears the mark of a tradition, a world of related concepts, a corridor of interpretation: rhizome. Sometimes that

7

history disappears: win-win.

Yet the word means less and less. In its journeys, its character becomes diffuse, its mechanism uncertain, its reputation sullied: culture. Sometimes we don't even realize that we are no longer talking about anything, that the thing to which the word once referred has left, even though the word still buzzes: power.

And She's Like

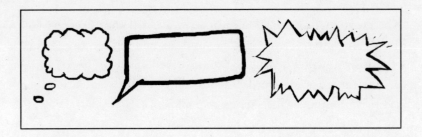

Young people these days, inarticulate and illiterate, a preverbal imprecision we should hope will not seriously be the future of our fair planet. 'I'm like', 'he's like', 'she's like'. What's become of the verb 'to say'?

'I'm like' crosses the separation of what is said and felt, what is expressed and understood. 'I'm like' is usually not what's said, but when he's like, 'fuck', then that's the meaning of his enunciative position in the context of the story. Subject positions registering how they are touched by affects, indicate what they want to say by stylized responses we can imagine the charming character of the story to have intoned. Even if no one actually said it.

Crackers Aren't Your Niggaz

Not because you can't reappropriate a word, not because you don't understand its historical and contemporary usage, not because you won't be true to the word's complex meaning; white people can't use the word nigga to refer to one another because the word has never threatened them.

That they can so easily reappropriate the words of others (especially African-Americans) is a habit establishing their privilege; that they understand the word's history is a result of an educated racial privilege; that they can simulate the word's meaning and invent for themselves a social validity to its function evidences the freedom white people enjoy to imagine their social condition.

It is because they have this freedom that they can and should use other words.

Acronyms

FUBAR.

Why use acronyms?

You can say more with fewer words: SNAFU (Situation Normal: All Fucked Up).

You make a reference that only insiders will understand: FTW (Fuck The World, in biker culture).

You want to abbreviate a frank but quite dreary name: IBM (International Business Machines).

You want a name no one else has, but you don't want to make it too weird: SDG&E (San Diego Gas & Electric).

You want a name that is both fanciful and serious: START (Strategic Arms Reduction Treaty).

Acronyms got old. Consumers retreat from a faceless collection of letters that, more often than not, stand only for a series of bland and misleading words. NATO (North Atlantic Treaty Organization), RAND (Research ANd Development), GMC (General Motors Company). The acronym just abbreviates meaninglessness. The acronym has offered refuge for those with something to hide, and this has hurt its reputation: the barely edible substances packaged as MREs are officially Meals Ready to Eat, but also known as Meals Rejected by Ethiopians.

What the people want now is not capital letters but word smooshes. PowerPoint, Starbucks, Facebook, Flickr, BevMo, Aquafresh, DreamWorks, Qualcomm. Random words are fine if they feel right, though they certainly don't have to mean anything: Tide, Target, Google, Apple, Cisco, Zappos, Pfizer. Deliberately misleading names are also in: Axe, Monster, LinkedIn, Microsoft Works.

Yet some acronyms remain: CVS, NBC, EPA, DOD, ATM, NYT.

Old things have good reasons to stay familiar.

You're Just Not Doing It Right

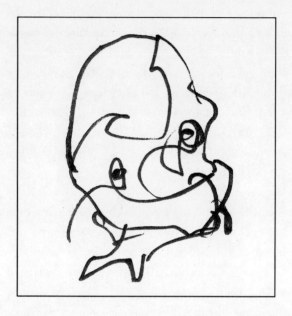

Couldn't you say that about anything? Getting rich, getting laid, getting a good job, getting the grades you want in school? It's not impossible, you're just not doing it right.

The expression makes individuals responsible for the outcomes of their actions, severely downplaying conditions and historical situation.

On the one hand, it's bullshit. It's an everyday performance of neoliberal responsibilization. We blame individuals for social problems and refuse to see personal struggles as expressions of structural conditions or as products of historical forces.

On the other hand, it makes a little bit of sense. Maybe you really are just not doing it right. This expression puts into words the truth that neoliberal ideology builds out from. (Or a truth that it connects with.)

The message is: it is not important if the world is wrong; you are wrong. But it's not personal. You are wrong because what you are doing is wrong. The problem is in what you are doing. You should do things differently and you would get better results. Maybe you should change your means, maybe you should change your self, maybe you should change your goals. The combination, all together, needs to be changed. There might be a right way that this can work. You're just not there yet.

It is doing, rather than individuals or social conditions, that decides whether things work. If things were done the right way, anything is possible.

Situations can be improved by reengineering your own actions, and we tell each other to focus on this perspective rather than contemplate what is difficult or unpleasant or tends to be likely or unlikely. You can start a small business and get rich, but if that hasn't worked (perhaps because you don't have a service to provide, have no business experience, or because the market is glutted or under monopoly control) you're just not doing it right. This is one way to look at the situation. We find this outlook compelling.

Superactually

Being polite, talking dirty, the gentle curtness of someone who is done talking with you. Voice lets us know how to take a remark. To speak superactually is serious business. It is just kidding and totally for real.

Superactually

Irony flaunts what it symptomatizes. 'GI Joe is a real American hero!' Satire performs symptoms so that its audience recognizes the problem through their shared revulsion. *A Modest Proposal*. We find ourselves as the audience that recognizes together. *The Colbert Report*.

Failure if we don't recognize. Failure if we are not repelled. Failure if we just enjoy.

A peculiar kind of vanilla sincerity presumes to be healthy, to express itself without symptomatizing something else.

Irony toys with escalating claims of sincerity: I'm so serious. That's how you let them know you're not serious, repeatedly insist that you are. Further degrees of irony are possible by adding inflections and ostensible commitments to this formula.

'No, I'm not joking, *The Little Mermaid* is really my favorite movie ever, I got a tattoo!'

'I'm serious that I was joking about not caring about dressing right'

'There's no meaning at all to this fine art gold sculpture of Michael Jackson'

Satire denies its place, forgets the world, and turns its topics virtual. We are engaged in a consideration of potentials, without agreeing on a specific underlying message which is real. I think what *The Onion* means, in their clip about Kafka International Airport, is that airports are alienating, confusing, and always Kafka-esque. But I'm not quite sure what that means, which airports, or how we experience this on most flights.

A post-ironic intensity symptomatizes as it expresses. It is superactual, a redoubling after a cynical recognition of the limit of sincerity. It is sick but keeps on living. It performs commitment to its explicit actual content (context suggests much of tone), yet encourages the audience to recognize its inability to overcome that which it symptomatizes.

Satire says what it does not mean in order to show what it wants very much to think. But it's often only possible to feel this confidence with ironic distance. Somehow, we know that GI Joe is not a real American hero, or that 'real American hero' is a vapid term capable only of describing GI Joe, but we need not agree with each other or ourselves to appreciate the ironic comedy.

The superactual tone includes ironic interpretation. Cynical reactions to it buzz around like parasites, it does not silence them, but surmounts their signifying semiotics. It is an alternative, a solution, a practical plan, yet also a kind of seriousness which many would-be satirists find themselves enacting by mistake.

Cynical Irony

Blade Trinity opens with a TV roundtable discussion of vampires in the city, with the police, talk show host, and a psychologist weighing in. The police deny there is a vampire problem, the trouble is the 'vampire hunter,' Blade, who is just a killer. The psychologist reminds us that anyone who believes in vampires is crazy and just trying to deal with their own sexual problems.

The film cuts to Blade killing off some low life vampires outside a warehouse. Vampires are real. Vampirism is not a perverse form of sexuality. Vampire bites do not stand in for necking, and are not a perverse dream of a sexuality whose function is reproductive of humans. Equally, interest in vampires is not a symptom of a closeted sexuality. Vampires bite people to feed the thirst, which is not a necessity or a hunger, but a physiological drive.

Cynicism is a condition of lost belief. An intellectual can no longer believe in vampires when he can understand them as superstition or, better, closeted homosexuality. You could be ironic without being cynical, but there's something particular about cynical irony.

Cynicism: 'vampires are a fantasy and not real.'

Irony: being killed by vampires you diagnosed as your subject's fantasy.

Cynical Irony: 'I'm afraid of vampires, especially their European accent.'

Cynical irony is a chummy suggestion that builds community on an idealism akin to anarchists' goal of no government or nihilists' goal of freedom beyond morality. The magic is to unstop the finality of truth as laziness. Nietzsche imagines truth as what we settle on when thinking and doubt end. Wherever they happen to end, that's truth. Cynical irony delivers us that kind of settled truth as a joke, because it's been exaggerated and put plainly, because it's been repeated crudely, because it's been made silly. Truth has been displaced, and as long as we are far from it, this is comforting. At least this terrible thing is not the bedrock of existence.

Community builds around this sort of speech because it seems strong in its apathy and purposeful in its rejection of old convention. Cynics habitually take what they hear with a grain of salt. '90% of everything anyone ever tells you is bullshit.' Hellboy is materially apathetic, his super power is that it never matters how he gets hurt (blown up, shot, dropped, crushed). He will always be ok, even if it hurts real bad. This is not the same as invincibility, but invincibility is the mechanism by which he achieves apathy. (You could be invincible but get knocked out, you could have a force field but still be scared.) The trick of apathy is an immunity to affect. A numbness. Cynicism's mechanism for apathy is itself, which displaces sensitivity to whatever sustains the cynicism.

Cynicism is very practical, refusing to make efforts with tools or beliefs that look unappealing. Irony's displacement of sincerity, however, opens the possibility of dumb irony. In a discussion of the glory of America's founding, a dumb ironic thing to say would be 'and they even treated the indigenous peoples so well that they would never be alcoholics, broke and selling trinkets on the side of the road!' This lets us off the hook of believing in America's glory, but it provides exactly a new stupid thing to believe: that most Indians are well characterized as indigenous people who are alcoholic and broke, that most are on the side of the road selling things, and that the things they sell are all trinkets.

Cynicism's tactic of irony offers a ward, a special protection. And perhaps by some strategy of irony, elusive cynicism, or indirect speech we can avoid a direct reckoning with the reality principle, but don't imagine you'll cut loose from the hyperreality principle. The ironic love of 80s cartoons is simulacral, it copies a nonexistent previous fandom. Cynicism does not have the generosity to give a (probably beastly and exclusive) proposition offering possibility. It regularly provides something less exciting but more practical, the friendly denial of something so wrong no one really had to argue the point.

Passive Voice

The passive voice also functions in games of concealing and revealing, to lay agency at someone else's doorstep in the night.

If there is a fabrication of subjectivities, power relations of subjugation, patternings of subjective experience, discourses that articulate a subject-as-topic, architectures realized in construction of subject positions, grammatical necessity to a subject, ideological definition of subjects to a master Subject, or a few of these in some combination. If these are not altogether different things. Entanglement.

Passive constructions are not a philosophical escape from a grammar infused with a metaphysics of the subject, wherein that subject is present and appears as an originary cause. (This power of the subject to take credit for miraculating predicates—theorized as free will debates, personal responsibility, cybernetic decentralization, or cellular automata—might be understood as a cause that, when viewed from the right angle, obscures other causes behind it.) Alternatives will not be found by the passive voice, but a reckoning may be forestalled. Subjectivity involves more than a grammatical subject that takes an object. Alternatives to the entanglement of subjectivity (or to some of its threads) most likely press out along different lines than a confrontation with a metaphysic present and alive 'in language.'

Not the reckoning: to delay a reckoning means avoiding encounters, minimizing interactions, keeping away from people and places, remaining silent on some issues, denying a place at the table to enemies. This is not a strategy for resistance, defiance, confrontation, revolution, or politics. It's a tactic, and a necessary one, for politics as housekeeping. The just man sweeps daily. Sweeping only moves the dirt around, and does not deal with the root cause of any of it.

Why use a solution if there is not a problem? The trick of passive voice to avoid an encounter is to provide wiggle room, to be slower to demand an answer. The point is that there is not a subject, or a thing in the place of the subject, no organization or individual, no single history or practice, that enacts the fabrication of the entanglement of subjectivity. But, how do we chronicle the implications of this agency without translating it again into a predicate in search of a subject?

Duplicity & Bullshit

A challenge of entering adulthood is parting with casual sincerity. It becomes necessary to willfully misrepresent yourself, but that's no longer how you should think about it. An applicant must be presented, a respectable adult must be costumed and performed, a friend must be mustered up, a colleague managed, a consensus reached. An adult body must be cultivated.

Bullshit isn't the same as lying, and lying is hardly more adult than childish. Bullshit is multiplying the conversation, influencing it, or making it discuss more than one thing at once. Bullshit engages different registers of different topics where we are different kinds of people. 'Spin' in politics allows people to say something that is, in one way, literally false, while, in another way, right on. To say there are two ways helps us imagine the dynamic of splitting and multiple engagements, but usually two is a simple case.

The duplicity of bullshit is the two-facedness of saying one thing that depends on what I know to be wrong but must treat as right in order to say something that we, then, no longer have the luxury of understanding as false. Was the framer's intent of the US constitution to allow gay marriage? If that's the fiction it takes to end that form of discrimination, we will stand for that shit like it's true.

Rarely can bullshit call itself bullshit, and that means denying other negotiations of the many terrains of discourse. Perhaps by calling all of them bullshit. Sincerity becomes incredibly difficult in adulthood, both as we fall out of practice, and as charting a course that remains true to our stance in each of many conversations becomes impossible, because we don't remember which poses we got into for what reasons. How could an authentic and natural self persist without our constant efforts at its reproduction and continuance?

Bullshit did not invent duplicity. It responds to a neurotic reality: too many conflicting rules so that we must lie to tell the truth, as Picasso said of art. Honest communication of minds conflicts with self-esteem and confidence, describing a situation can change it, our own strategic map of relationships might lose its power when shared with those involved. Expressions cannot expect to be true or false all the time, because they are necessarily burdened with being more than that (thank god).

Truth and falsity depend on practices of verification to maintain their meaning, but those practices are themselves part of the world we engage in.

Apparently

Apparently he was angry about it. Not that it matters to whom he seemed angry. We could talk about why. But what the word asks for first is confirmation. Appearances function as truth, which is why the construction does not ask for the audience to deny false impressions. Instead it asks for alliance against a social reality for which the appearance is not false.

A paranoid pact against those others who see wrongly and believe through how things merely seem. A respectful and knowing glance to those who will agree to deny what is apparent, from a body that turns back to those visions it struggles constantly to deny but never can. An idealism that envisions our rebel alliance against their flighty and weak tendency to believe.

But also, the suggestion that maybe we can make something of this appearance, that we need not dismiss or forget it.

Real Secrets

Most secrets we're dying to share so we can make allies against what is apparently true. Others are open secrets, part of everyday duplicity. But the truly secret is kept secret by means that are themselves kept secret.

Secret secrets are the dark matter of social life. How large or important are they? How many are there? Where are they? When you stumble upon something that is not to be shared, when you realize something that is true but should be kept quiet exactly because it is true. Sometimes these secrets have an important and widespread consequence, but one that is not to be revealed. Secrets of a trade, secrets of a community, secrets of a race. They are images or understandings of how things work or what things are, but they are representations kept silent.

Most of what we call secrets are things we are willing to talk about, and thus name as 'secrets.' Usually people are eager to share these secrets, to an appropriate confidant. These common secrets help hide the existence of darker secrets that are not even named secrets. The very acknowledgment of a secret is a hint. This risks its disclosure.

Secrets that we want to share we think of often. The truly secret we can even manage to forget, to think of rarely.

Because real secrets prefer not to be confirmed, we can only happen upon them by intuition, imagination, and serendipity. Knowing that there exist real secrets, that things are not as they appear, that there is some dark thing which prefers not to be named, is an impetus to think through feeling.

Hype

It's something in the air. Pure hype. Everyone wants a browser, a bundle, to get their toolbar installed with an opt-out provision on the software that transforms the HP Pavilion some guy bought for cheap in a package deal into the computer he was hoping for. To monitor. To know where you go, what links you make, what cookies you accumulate, what search terms you enter, how much time you are online, how long you stay at a site: a complete record of online behavior. To figure out how to profit. They don't want or need or even hope to control the user, not at this time; that will come on its own. They will convert investor money into personal riches, wealth for the company, charitable donations, steady streams of income.

The hype will make good. It won't just be advertising supporting advertising, it will be etailing, ecommerce; the infrastructure for our way of life will move online (as it has) and they will be the Mall to our suburban teenage social scene.

A grand plan, a long shot, an inevitability whose realization they work assiduously to ensure. Until then, there is hype. In the fullness of time, in the next age, in the near future, in the next moment of late capitalism, it won't be hype. It won't be the future, it will then be the present.

Hype functions to pave the way for this realization, but is also the primary nature of the industry at this point in time. It is potential, where things might go, a direction or a kind of latent energy. The hype has sustained itself for years, through many companies, between business models, amidst devastating evidence to the contrary. And it isn't primarily a dream; there's no necessary or single utopian model in the hype, and little reason to believe those dreams will ever take form as the hype suggests.

Hype nominates something as cool. When we see something cool, we do the hype. When we hear the hype, we might want to check it out. I suggest to others that they enjoy what I have enjoyed, I expect that they will do the same for me.

Hype is auditory, it's a hubbub (Twitter in 2007), it emits wild screams (M.I.A. after her first album), it can only sometimes be heard from far away (Thaitanium), it echoes (it is 'viral'), it surrounds something which is real, but it has no body: it is a vibration, a disturbance, a real phenomenon, but lacking substance or materiality in the sense of traditional sculpture. Permanence, solidity, presence, opacity, form, and weight? No.

But the hype coordinates, attracts, incites, deforms, deters, guides, influences, questions, popularizes, neglects, denies, or lifts. It is not a body hewn of earth, but it may be a prevailing wind.

Hype tends to build on non-knowledge, ignorance, misunderstanding. How excited we are about bright fresh new things with which we've not yet spent long hours getting familiar.

Hype predicts what will be the future, and so enacts the arrival of an immediate future, that is thereby also the present rather than any more the future. Bigger shoulders, bright orange for men, neon for everyone, tablets, and Senegalese mashups. Expecting them, they take form already. Knowing them, they are no longer the future but just trends in the present.

Semiotize by Function

Semiotics is the study of signs. It explores the traffic and habits of meaning. The Hindenburg disaster means something. It means many things to many people and meaning is the medium by which all kinds of little things touch all the other things in the world. That's the basic idea of semiotics.

What semiotics does is read things. It turns situations, objects, materials, encounters, experiences, and practices into texts and relations of reading.

This translates all activity into signification. Smoking a cigarette, eating candy, making a speech, signing a contract, making a joke. Rather than doing something or being just as simple as they seem to those at the scene, they mean something. (They mean something generally and to those at the scene as well, even if unconsciously.) Such an approach tends to downplay feelings ('affect') and materiality, even as it depends upon materiality for its own claim to significance. (The newspaper headline is real ink on real pages in the real hands of people reading its text.)

This habit that goes too far is a stultifying theory, a productive method for honed thought. It returns inevitably to ideology, identification, the grammar of subjectivity, hermeneutics, a kind of associative rationality, problematics of reappropriation, and difference.

The technique of semiotization is to create a complicated map from some stuff that might not otherwise be interesting. (A pasta ad.) Making these maps complicated is the very definition of rigor: the more considerations you express sensitivity to, the more legitimate your writing is. Sea World relative to race, class, gender, environmentalism, amusement parks, the entertainment industry, television, nature documentaries, public space.

To semiotize by function is to understand things by how they function, rather than by what they mean. The emphasis is on how rather than what. Answers to 'how' questions tell of mechanisms, kinds of influence, arrangements of power, dynamic activity, interactions, styles, conditions, effects, and adverbs. 'What' questions are answered by images, essentialized concepts, comparisons, references, ongoing developments, clear practices, processes or procedures, precisely defined patterns, and the ineffability of experience.

This is one way to describe much of what I've written here. As semiotics focuses too much on meaning because it is unable to imagine what matters beyond it, I find myself stuck on function.

Being Affected By Feelings

Whatever cannot be represented by one set of techniques will eventually become the thing that is most interesting to represent. Today, it is not culture or language, but affect. Feelings, and their peculiar ability to influence things, feel pressing.

Emotional/Intellectual

Usually the emotional and intellectual go hand in hand. Thinking and feeling match. Don't abuse animals. If you are hungry, eat. Say hello to your friends.

For a particular person, does one dominate the other? Personality tests say yes.

For people en masse, can one tendency overwhelm the other?

If you reject the distinction between thought and feeling, you don't have to deny that thinking happens and that some responses involve very little (of what might be counted as) thought. Like pornography, thought can exist without being defined.

(For the Myers-Brigg test, thinking itself is rational and feeling seeks harmony. I do not consider thinking, as an activity, to be capable of rationality and do not see feelings as naturally driven toward comfortable agreement.)

Thought and feeling can enlist one another. To an extent, rationalization is excuses. That is to say, thought can follow feeling. 'I do feel strongly about it, I think the reason is that…' And, in other cases, we find ourselves obliged to find emotional truth in what we recognize we should do. Feeling can follow thought. 'You just have to get used to the idea that…'

If the two activities involve each other, thinking is the combination and weighing of different feelings against each other.

Thinking is the mechanism of the uncertainty of ambivalence. Each feeling is a valence. Emotion is a dressed up feeling, presentable to the world. Yet this cannot be fully distinguished from a feeling, because it is the form by which feelings express themselves and are made the object of other feelings.

Most people, in some moments, act in a way that does not make sense (generate something they can assimilate as a sense).

Most people, in some moments, act in a way that does not feel so good (a smooth motion resulting in a sensation).

Which are you?

The mixing and pushing of feelings against one another is thinking. Passion is when a set of feelings breaks away and forces thought to follow. Over-thinking it is when you can no longer feel the feelings.

If our world is particularly saturated with affect, if the management of affect is the impossible chore we find occupying our institutions and personal lives, thinking (in its diverse styles) is sometimes a mediating process by which affects affect us.

Seven Thousand Senses

With our eyes, we can see. With our ears, we hear. With the nose one can smell. Where do we touch or feel?

The muscles themselves register weight but it is nerves that feel cramps. A different set of nerves detect temperature, and particular parts of tissues sensitive to vibrations notice when your cell phone rings on silent. The body has a sense of its own location in space. This is called proprioception. Is it, again, through the sense of touch that I feel exhausted or ready to go, nervous or hungry? What perceives pleasurable touch, orgasm, or comfort?

The human ability to sense the surrounding environment does not break down into five distinct categories, each associated with a particular organ.

There are differences within organs: we can see brightness with our eyelids shut, night vision detects colors differently and uses different photoreceptors from regular vision, peripheral vision is very responsive to movement but lacks any of the clarity of the fovea.

One sense often involves more than one organ: we can hear bass rumbling in our bones, feel a whoosh of air with the tiny hairs on our skin, watch a person's mouth to see how it is forming the words that we think we simply hear.

There are senses that have no exclusive claim on any organ: a sense of dread, a sense that someone is lying to you, a sense of time, a sense of loss, a sense of humor.

Yet these are all senses. They are faculties by which the body perceives external stimuli.

Blocks of Sensation

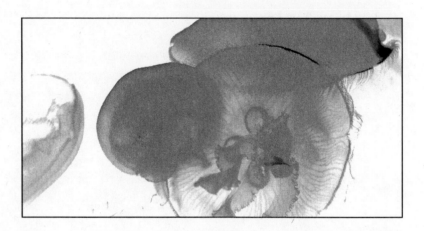

Blocks of sensations are units of what can be experienced or felt that may have limits but are not necessarily defined by them. (Similarly, a forest may end abruptly at a lake in one place, but peter out into brush elsewhere.) Affect, in the sense used by Deleuze and Guattari, is sculpted of blocks of sensation.

Sometimes, often when half-asleep, my fingers feel wide and fat, my hands feel heavy, there is no detail to their sense of touch; they are ham hands, but warm and strong, almost unbreakable, as if made of rubber. Certain sensations are blocked out: if the fingers have fallen asleep, the feeling of pressure, what they are touching. Other are blocked together: the warm temperature, their own mass, the fingers' nearness to each other. It's the same way with armor or blue jeans, there is always some numbness in the segmentation of perception (as in scale).

Affect, in this sense, is a content (like a fortune in a fortune cookie) that is a substance (like clay) which gives form (like wavy hair). Affect may be a flow or a pulse, a mass or a modicum. (Continuous or discrete, a field or particle.)

None of this vocabulary aims to quite represent emotions that are

36

fragile and delicate. Critics worry this vocabulary forces the indescribable texture of reality to shrink even further from thought, by exposing even it to a language of logic and signification. I disagree. This is a way to describe throughput, institutions, planning, zones, mediums, masses, uncountable liquids, immeasurable solids. A single cell protein combined with synthetic aminos, vitamins, and minerals. It fetishizes machines.

The language of affect functions as a consolidation and strategic misrepresentation (codeword) of human feeling, to deterritorialize it from molar formations* (theories, formulas, Hallmark). Real emotion occurs interpersonally and its representations (molar forms) are as important as whatever affects subtend it. Affect may be a kind of material input for machines, but it can also be a stimulus for intelligences, or impetus for thinking. Pick the metaphor that challenges you more, and imagine affect that way, because it still aims to challenge the imagination.

It does not capture our most intimate particles in the staid and imperial language of logic and scholarship, subjecting it to that cycle of fashion, standard of rigor, infighting, bickering, and criteria of clarity and teachability. Although, if theorizing affect could simply be called a step, it would be a step in that direction.

A block of sensation is also what keeps one theoretical understanding of a topic from letting the topic go, from relenting in its interrogation, in its pursuit of the truth presumed to lie within the topic. Given a theoretical approach, new developments confirm it, deny it, evidence changes within it, suggest redistribution of its components, or shifts in its proportions. Thus, changes must be historical ones, and they result in increases and decreases, or shifts, but never in the release of something. The old terms have become, not just jargon or pig-paths of thinking, but the blocks of sensation by which the affect of the thing to be studied can reach us. Put your head in a bucket until you can see the stars inside.

* One aspect of a molar formation is that it may be a block of sensation, which is an apt description of that happiness which in others we are always attempting to probe.

Awesomeness

Intense. Shocking. A bit overwhelming. Unexpected.

Often not relaxing or kind or tasteful or pleasing.

Awesome is different from fly, chill, wizard, wicked, cool, groovy, neat, and swell.

Each term indicates a degree of intensity (or importance) that is a blank endorsement. To say any of these words is to perform an affirmation.

But each word also connotes a sensibility.

A favorite word of approval indicates something about the context where it flourishes. (A region, a people, or a moment.) It betrays what is considered good, even as it explicitly gives an approval devoid of semantic meaning. By saying something is cool, I am not interpreting the thing, I am approving it without describing it. Or so it seems, but neutrality emerges from general agreement.

That we like awesome, for those who do, shows we enjoy intensity, flare, and effect. Neat implies something that fits, contributes to the bigger picture, and has a tidy style. A thing can be called tight when there is no excess, no need for improvement, and no getting by it. Something sick is out of the ordinary, almost offensively good, perversely nice. Something bad is worthy of approval because it refuses what is boring and square so well, so righteously.

Interesting

'I don't know whether I'm for it or against it, but it certainly is provocative!'

To say something is interesting is to say that it is enjoyable in a particular way. What is that particular way?

When something is interesting it can be mild and nice or exciting and challenging. But this feeling can only be painted on a very neutral canvas. When you're in a receptive state. What's merely interesting gets ignored if one is terrified, despondent, or overjoyed. *If* there is nothing more important, *then* interesting matters.

This condition is emotional and material: I don't have anything more pressing, I have the time, I am not distracted by hunger, I am in a calm and open mood, there is not too much else going on.

The neutrality that is a precondition for 'interesting' to mean 'enjoyable' is not just comfort, but also curiosity (which we might call 'will'), the potential for future extrapolation and application (a point, or more exactly purposivity), and an enthusiasm to pose as one who is interested (readiness to become a person who is interested).

This describes the quality and reaction (combined) that we know as the interestingness of a thing, something being interesting.
'That's very interesting.'

What makes something interesting? Limited intelligibility; a deformation of what is ordinary; a sensed potential for novel and appealing interaction; qualities that one would like to dwell on; or desirability as a topic of conversation.

You don't know exactly what is so interesting, but you want to find out.
That something is interesting suggests a possible pleasure that depends on the context where it's encountered and the state of the one who enjoys it. When something's interesting, you want more.

That Ruled

Tigers fighting. BMX tricks on fire. Practical jokes played perfectly.

It's very hard to modify the phrase 'that ruled' because its meaning is exclusively idiomatic. A movie that ruled was sovereign over nothing, had no government or policies.

It may have dominated our experience at the time, so it feels like it overpowered everything else around us. But we don't say 'that ruled all of you!' or 'that ruled the whole crowd.'

The usual modifier is a simple increase of intensity: 'That ruled so hard.' Or, written by hand, 'That Ruled.' Underlined.

Why do we accept and use the phrase? There are other words we hear and do not pick up. Probably because something about it rules.

Organized Affect

Why is everyone talking about affect? We are bitter because emotion is served to us, processed and packaged, with its effect anticipated and accounted for as profit, as changing our state, as customer satisfaction, as plausibility, as persuasion.

To respond, we seek the primitive basis for packaged emotion and experience. The raw substance of feeling: affect. Affect is an impulse that affects bodies, it is the ineffable quantum (or wave) by which things interact, relations occur.

But to concentrate on this, in strict contradistinction to emotion (as if the two could be separated and should be), is to miss key aspects of feeling.

Affect puts subjects (who we can define now as those subject to affect) in moods. Moods prefer some feelings to others, and therefore are more receptive to some feelings and more likely to discover them. A mood for joy, for destruction, for calmness.

That which changes a mood is not always affect. Anger can be burnt up by expressions of rage (tearing up cardboard). Self-doubt can become nervousness that lingers or dissipates. Thought can change a mood. So can a change of situation. Even a short walk can begin to change ones perspective on shit.

Moods (affective states) are idealized forms and individuals experience and express them differently. Not all moods are possible for all subjects, though, for anyone, a mood can be identified and then developed into something resembling a mood. That is, to be recognized as a mood requires the mood be translated or organized into something legible as a mood. 'Nobody understands me' is the prehistory to such moods. But then the sensibility must be trained into a legible mood.

The term affect suggests that feelings are not strictly psycho-logical, not just subjective and opposed to the world which is itself only objective. Instead, the objective world exists through objects experiencing one another subjectively. Affect is the generic means of the processual occurrence of the world. (Whitehead's term prehension is close.)

Affect radiates from phenomena, but represents an event reductively. There is always more to what happens than how it makes one feel, than how it strikes one.

Sensitivity is trained, elaborately, and in conjunction with one's self-familiarity. One learns to feel and learns how to feel about feeling and also one develops unconscious habits of response.

I get a bad vibe from a lecturer, but that is not all. I know I am too harsh on lecturers in general, that we are all tired, that the audience is unresponsive, that she is making jokes at our expense. I have nothing to gain by noting her faults, except credi-bility from those who suffer with me. I keep calm and carry on. But I do not smile; I distract myself by reading or thinking something else. I change my posture to make myself comfortable with the situation, crossing my legs or leaning back. (These defensive postures may ultimately cause physical discomforts that agitate the anxieties that drive me to the postures.)

Affect is structuring. It does not build order or systems. It joins with other feelings, already existing or that are only possibilities on the horizon. It overpowers some, triggers others, forms into amalgams, affects different parts of the body. It is not primitive and it is not entirely organized.

Making Sense of What is Happening

When you realize there is a pattern, when you sense there is something more important to be said, when you are shut down by someone with persuasive words, when you want to tell someone else that their crazy rules do not apply.

Rational Thinking

Rationality is not thought. Or, rationality is not a kind of thinking experienced subjectively. It is a set of forms for creative output and thereby also an inspiration for an imagination. Don't find reason in the brain. It isn't even in what we say about what's in the brain; it's a genre of creative production. Like book covers or trading cards. Mostly stylistic conventions, but never without fragments of an interpretive community.

These forms for rational output (hypothesis-data, claim-warrant-evidence, etc.) might stay alive through expressions, but they are principally ground for critique. A bunch of mistakes you might have made, a uniformed service for some kinds of discourse. Rationality in business, rationality in parenting, rationality in social policy, rationality for restaurateurs, rationality for free inquiry.

Something So Wrong

I *like* to hear something incorrect when it makes me immediately want to correct it. People with good IQ scores are smarter and therefore more valuable to society. Fuck that noise!

What's impossibly hard is to hear something so wrong that I forget what is right. The very wrong thing blocks access to what is right, and, feeling that this is unfamiliar territory, my position in conversation is to accept ('provisionally') what is grossly wrong until I find why it is wrong. Otherwise I disagree without being able to explain why.

Something that's wrong often resembles something right: it feels familiar, it applies anesthesia to the area.

Don't throw your knife away! A life for a life. It will blow your pants off. India was better off after colonization than it was before.

The first rhymes with something true; the second uses a mathematical/logical structure to justify the (very unequal) death penalty with equality; the third is wrong, but can you remember the correct expression? The fourth example suggests a very complicated discussion about world history and local changes over several centuries can be reduced to a before and after comparison, but then, lacking another approach, isn't this an insightful and true comment?

Something so wrong can do more than false information or illogical construction do. It can weaken the listener so that something that could have been said before is no longer accessible. Is the death penalty fair? Was colonization a good thing for India? These questions, unlike the wrong statements given above, are much easier to respond to.

A statement can be phrased to deny dialogue with another

person's (often well-trained) instincts. This is a powerful thing about saying something so wrong. Let it strike others as wrong, but watch as they fumble for an answer.

Cynicism as Method

Method does not happen once, it is not content to rest, but can be applied recursively, reflectively, repetitively, ridiculously. As a method, cynicism reveals wisdom and knowledge we did not know we had by drawing it out with statements we come to recognize as false. How does it work?

Confronted with a question, I take a first reaction, usually one that's snarky. Snarkiness, without reason, is irritating and indefensible. In responding to a thing, it assumes that thing is wrong. The brilliance of cynicism (and snarkiness) is that it suggests a new reason that it might not have known before. This reason appears, and is the place where work and creativity begin. Think of cars.

Initial take: Cars are important to people and the way we get to the places that we're going.

Quick response: Cars are really fantastic and everyone just loves them! They're important to places that need people to get to them, and cars place people in important goings.

Like an algorithm that needs random numbers to seed it, a response must appear, more or less by chance. Here, instincts in the face of uncertainty improvise a creative response. There are many tactics and they share with comedy an originality of language that disappears in written texts. Off the cuff remarks. Getting carried away. That is one tactic. Another is wordplay, turning verbs into nouns, swapping subjects and predicates. There are others. They can be silly, they are often trendy (adding the word embodiment or pluralizing nouns), they are sometimes well-respected (etymology or historical juxtaposition).

The response above suggest a line of argument: Cars let places command people while giving those people the impression that they're very important because they are the ones who are mobile (an idea they like). Cars are probably not a good experience for many people and are very poorly understood as 'useful,' perhaps because their function tends to be given rather than chosen. (It would also be misleading to say that a heart or ID card is useful; they are most useful to those who steal them, and simply necessary to most of us.)

Apply the method again: Are you so ready to accept that we're dominated by an invisible and unidentified force that you would deny our palpable, if inconsistent, enthusiasm for automobiles? How can a place 'command' anything?

Repeat as necessary.

This method is, like deconstruction, always concerned about being too naive. This method is, like dialectics, obsessively involuting theses. This method is, like improv comedy, always ready to throw everything out the window and take the next step. This method does not guarantee full coverage; not once in this discussion of cars did it come up that they are deadly.

Stultifying Theory

Sometimes social theory stultifies the possibilities of a concept or a thing. Sometimes with good reason. Racism means social and historical reality, not just stereotypes or insensitive words. Sexuality is a specific discursive construct that emerged over a number of years in Western Europe. Software is something used in everyday life, not just a stretch of code unbridled by dominant use or interpretation. Birds are basically animals that live in nature and not just drawings, sound effects, pets, or sources of meat.

Renaming is one technique of theory, and one response to it. Other names may remind us why researchers are 'knowledge workers' or elephants are 'charismatic megafauna.' But theorization is more unrelenting than renaming is. Shifting attention to other things is another key trick: a movie plays in a particular theater, a recipe resembles lists and receipts as a form of writing, a flavor has certain effects that define it better than its creators can. Aligning a thing with other concepts of it can be quite powerful even when working with materials that are no match for a theory's conceptual apparatus. Oppose psychoanalytic practice to animatronics; compare anthropological and humanist concepts of culture to yogurt; respond to Cartesian dualism with My Bloody Valentine. (Three examples from *Doom Patrols*.) These are possible responses to theories that make concepts tired and nail down what is always moving.

Stultification makes a thing available to other things. It reduces (as a sauce is reduced, or as a knife cuts something down to size) unspeakable complexity that is without a name to a thing. Usually to a kind of thing. An ideal case, a diagram, a practice, a set of general rules, or a procedure. That a thing is of a known kind helps us process it, although different methodological moments have treated their reductions differently. 1960s American academic Marxism made objects of research into parts of Capitalism's function as a system. 1990s postmodernism made topics fluid, multiple, and open to profound change by fresh interpretation. Deleuzian concepts are potentials actualized in creative new ways for each case.

When I want to say what a thing is, I want to prepare it for use. But what kind of use? A miniature for a diorama, an algorithm for a process, an image for a collage, a name for a list. Stultification makes one thing part of a broader interpretation, and thus constrains the one thing in order that other things might move and change. Or, stultification expands a tiny detail into a brigade on which we will now ride out to meet the sun.

The production of banners (backed by intricate representing-machines with many moving parts) is not always such a bad thing. Responses abound, and to every simplification complexity can be reintroduced. Indeed, adding complexity is exactly the mechanism of simplification, for theory. 'Making it more complicated that it has to be,' streamlines it for function. There are also those who claim that stultification is an error that can be avoided, a limit that can be transcended. I will reduce them to another case of the same dynamic: this rhetoric of truth always promises a new means of verification, a new truth procedure, a new play-set where we can put reductions suitable for it. Usually by envisioning a new map of what remains in our reach but beyond our grasp.

Many Constructions

It's not about social construction *versus* reality, but about a multiplicity of discourses where various representations and simulations relate to each other in different ways. The rain storm is simulated on the computer, presented as an icon in the newspaper, avoided by the traveler, welcomed by the gardener, added to the total amount of rain for the month and year, watched from the mountains, and welcomed by children who play in it. The reality of the rain storm comes about (is 'constructed') in a way that is sometimes social, but also sometimes mathematical, optical, emotional, or economic. The way that rain forms in clouds, the way that rain clouds form, the way that any of this is modeled, the way that the modeling is discussed, planned, or paid for are different.

The more socially constructed something is, the more real it is. However, the reality constructed may not be the same in its everyday practice as it is when it is imagined. Nuclear weapons are politically radical in their actual detonation, boringly conservative in their disciplinary function (the hydrogen bomb, the nuclear threat, the nuclear umbrella, deterrence, protocol for civilian responses to nuclear emergencies), yet disruptive as 'nukes,' an insensitive word that understands the threat of a pensive political situation.

We don't have access to most processes of construction. Rain forming in clouds? The snowmelt that starts a river? Fusion reactions in the sun?

We engage, as we can, with those constructions that may respond to us best.

Rational Human Nature

It has long been a dream to find a fixed human nature with which to make claims about social reality. Humans are essentially greedy and violent. Or, people are naturally inclined to share and live together peacefully.

In any complexity with a social dimension, human nature would be a set of properties that predict future behavior. These properties guard arguments against the possibility of human exceptions. The wily humans could be counted on to do one thing right: act according to their nature.

Visions of human nature fail because behavior is complex and varied. Complex because we are greedy while trading but generous with friends of the family. Varied because there are different traditions and individuals and cultures and styles (macro-variation). Varied again (micro-variation) by mood and weather and considerations which are obvious to the human actor, but often invisible to an outside observer (or unanticipated by those modeling behavior).

A more flexible concept is necessary to do the work of human nature. This concept can be arrived at by closely observing behavior as a large set of intentional acts. These accounts compliment the subjects of a study. They are very understanding. Impulse buys make sense. Sharing, religion, and morality are all practiced for reasons those reading about studies can relate to, not for strange or untranslatable local reasons.

This does not mean that rational actors have been understood as unemotional or disembedded, only that their behavior is, in every case, somehow understandable, rather than inexplicable. The argument that rational actor theory is wrong because people are 'not rational' mistakes an image of thinking (rationality) for a process of thinking. It is the explanation of an action that is rational, not the actor's own thinking. The question is not 'Am I Rational?' but 'Could I be Represented as Rational?' Insofar as you are what you do, then you can be treated as always already (interpellated as) a rational actor. Another subject rendered in a rational sound.

This whole mode is the opposite of cultural anthropology, where cultures give people the impetus to act. Rational decision making, it seems, does not follow any rules but those of the conditions at hand.

Humans described by anthropology act because of customs and habit, within a confined range of options. They act in a way that those reading the ethnography can just barely understand. If the natives are rational, it is a foreign rationality, an alien intelligence.

The rationality of a rational actor is partial and specific. But it is partial to what seems neutral and specific to what we readily accept as universal.

To question the rational actor model, and the work it does as a substitute for more embarrassing theories of human nature, we can: divide identity from observed action, emphasize what is partial and specific about the rationality used in explaining behavior, insist upon the ubiquity of unknown unknowns in every situation, and/or compete rhetorically with the accounts of behavior that are so easily accepted as rational.

The Untheorized

'I have a theory.' That is the diagram.

In the past that is a virtual time distinct from the present with its opening into a particular imagination of the future, there is a wild prehistory to every theory. They had only their instincts to guide them. This past virtualizes a theory's present, but also demands its coming into being. It is the time from which the theory emerges, and it is a romantic backstory for the theory. Before speech act theory, people saw dimly how they might sometimes do a thing with words.

In the sense that the theory is contemporary, all else is its past; on the map that this temporal function effects, there lie dragons. Those who understood, saw clearly, worked within their conditions towards what change lay within reach. Those who practiced what the theory calls for, before there was the theory to name its calling. Those theories, mighty enough in their own times and places, against which the new theory is to be considered an improvement, an update, a redesign.

An extra moment for this last movement: a theory remembers its past as other theories. Before my theory of the discrete charm of automobile commuting, there are others. Aside from the Marxist theory of imprisonment, there are folk theories. Everyone has a theory of the self, at all times. These moments, sometimes having pronounced themselves as theories, but usually not, are no longer the untheorized when accounted for in this way. They are competitors for the niche of the theory. They would occupy the same site, service the same connecting cities, be used with the same supplies.

We contemporary subjects, each ourselves in the first person, but pluralized by the universalization of the theory as a mode of

practice, each animate the theory by presenting, recalling, carica-
turing, deploying, modifying, or teaching its system. Each I of the
we meets the ever changing present with the theory's division of
latent and manifest, knowable and forgettable, expression and
content. Likewise, this we has a way of not knowing its past
which, in the voice of each speaker whom the theory rides,
segments perception of the past with a numbness to the untheorized.

For that untheorized that is not equal to its representation in a
theory's entourage, there is no we that gives it voice. Who might
defend the omnifarious perspectives, techniques, knowledges,
and practices which are presently imagined by the theory as that
for which it substitutes? Who represents the chaos that (we now
claim) came before? The untheorized does not amount, it does
not amount to anything, it is scraps that are not fragments of one
whole between them all, but of many events in the occurrence of
which the untheorized subsists.

Yet, the untheorized is not only the past. It can be the core of a
discourse. For those who don't meditate, it is easy to ask what
meditation is. But for practitioners, any answer to this question is
at best a point of departure or a simple answer for others. Any
particular theory is only another gateway to the practice of
meditation. In this case, as with humor for comedians, the untheorized is the unfinished vitality at the center of a thing.

In this chaos that is full of structures, the tendential wilderness of
the untheorized, exists the practical wisdom of many approaches
that have been effective, clever, unjustified, and sufficient for
various projects in many times and places. Theories crossed the
chaparral before the railroad came.

Agency

Agency is a locus of attention, a zone with expectations, a body entitled to do things. Watch the senators. The battlefield will decide. The IMF acts.

Theory gives you agency, tells you where and how you have an ability to act.

Paying attention to something, as in paying attention in school, means ignoring what you were attending to before. Forgetting the glints of light dancing on the ceiling.

Concept, Tool, Reason

Arm of Dr. Cynthia Taylor

Talking of concepts, we become frustrated. What are they for? Let us speak only of a difference that makes a difference. Now our concepts will be useful. They have become tools.

Tools, unlike mere ideas, are actionable. They let us do things. We can accomplish outcomes, and this utility authorizes the concept. By outcome, or by reference to outcome (which is different), economics can make claims about human behavior without either psychological or philosophical rigor. Looking to its accomplishments, how sternly can we denounce first wave feminism?

Mischaracterization, fallacy, or the play of concealing and revealing are essential to concepts or arguments. A death penalty supporter's sign reads, 'A LIFE FOR A LIFE.' By a displacement of what is nonsensical, we have a concept whose clarity and sense serve an agenda.

So, the concepts (as tools) let us do what we want! Excellent. But what do we want to do? Really, how are we to imagine what we want to do if everything we can think of is just a tool?

There is another power of concepts: they are seductive. There is a fatal power beyond what they offer for our discriminating use. When you have a hammer everything starts looking like a nail. Capacities become relations, tools are also artifacts, tricks of argument become reasons to do things. Ideas are reasons and not just tools. We get a purpose from what were supposed to be techniques and it's not just a better mousetrap, it's a new campaign of trapping mice. Concepts are tools are reasons.

Stop. Don't let an idea turn into something else; forget its foreign affairs, its world to change.

Apprehended in their form, reasons are no more than concepts. They have internal relations, structure, substance, maybe consistency, and a logical method. They are little machines, movements, prepared strategies, manners, or elegant sculptures. If they don't make sense, we might forget them. If they are ugly and wrong, incorrect and out of date, just move on.

But a concept cannot live by itself. Understandings of its form are not fixed, and often terrible, old white guy ideas are radical and life changing to those who have never heard them before.

Whenever mobilizing concepts and presenting under-standings of their form, concepts become reasons. There is a reason to think what I say is true. We get a purpose from ideas.

Many thinkers hope desperately that their formulations become reasons, purposes, noble goals. Or that the ideas have, encoded into them, a political compass to collaborate with righteous goals. But more often, thinkers are arms merchants, perfecting their concepts only to have them appropriated for whatever against their wishes. Tool ideas fighting on the wrong side of battles on the other side of the world.

Because ideas become tools in their use, reasons (which can be post hoc or an impetus) convert many ideas into a set of tools for maneuvering or keeping an argument. A particular function apprehends things as a functional aspect. You are a pawn in her game; not a tiny flame maker but a cigarette lighter. The movement of reason interacts with a tool aspect of what is also just an idea. Yet, despite all this, tools and reasons can remain vulnerable to comments about them as concepts.

Entertainment

Entertainment gives experiences to bodies, usually of relaxation and mild, pleasant feelings. Machines automate this production of experiences, customers select between them, businesses capitalize on the ritual.

How Video Games Matter

Ok, video games are big money. In 2008, the buzz was that the industry would soon become larger than film, with gross revenues larger than music. This didn't happen, but the idea has an afterlife; it's evidence that video games are an important cultural phenomenon.

Here is the question. Does the fact that video games involve *more money* mean they are *more important*?

Does more money spent mean more people played? Dividing sales revenue by the cost of a particular game shows how many copies sold. But revenue will never tell you how many people played a game, because it can only tell you how many copies were sold *new* (not resale) and *legally* (not downloaded, borrowed, or copied illegally). Probably revenue indicates the minimum number of players, though buying something doesn't always mean you will use it. If you want to argue that loads of people play games, the revenue numbers are weak because they overemphasize expensive games. Most games people play are cheap or free. Solitaire, Snake, Facebook games. This is especially true for players who are not young men.

Second, the revenue numbers are not a good indicator of the *priority* of one medium over another. There is no definite way to compare industries, and only counting box office sales of movie tickets is not an effective way to judge how much money a movie made. Even if more people spend as much time playing games as watching movies, we still don't know which experience *influences* them more. For raw hours, TV is still king.

Third, that video games have big numbers proves they are expensive. Freely converting between currencies means ignoring national contexts. Reference to revenues will always overstate the behavior of countries with stronger currencies and higher prices.

Spending by one German person will outweigh ten customers in rural India. Things done by Londoners and Muscovites will be most important, if we treat dollar signs as cultural impact. That's sensible for business, but does it warrant the claim that video games are somehow important culturally?

Should we pay more attention to what young men in the overdeveloped world do with their free time than what other people do?

A statistic is an interesting number, which is why statistics lie. They don't have to be meaningful for the right reason; they can interesting for any reason. 12% of the US workforce has worked at McDonald's. The fact is free standing, interesting by itself, and potentially misleading. We want the pretty factoid to matter, even though the terms that give it meaning are irrelevant (Who is the workforce? What's the average length of employment at McDonald's?).

What does it mean to say that video games 'matter?'

The old standard was art: if video games are art, then they are worthy of intelligent discussion. The new paradigm is entertainment: if this is what people are plugging into, then this is where they're getting their brainwashing and spending their time?

What ought to establish the priority of a medium or activity for social thought? What does establish importance? If we believe that a cultural activity influences most the group most engaged with it, golf is a very crucial activity because the power elite play it. But if what matters is the metaphors that guide decision making, football is probably tops. If activities matter because they are simply how people spend their time, then having drinks and complaining about work is the key site of cultural life in most of the world. Finally, if media are interesting because of their content alone and it doesn't matter who is paying attention, then analysis of games will be more original and potentially powerful if the game is obscure.

A different approach is to identify continuities between games and software, web design, power, and life. Rather than the money spent buying things that will someday be other things, it is the continuities themselves that make games matter.

First World Color

Black hoodies, white tile, beige buildings, red plastic chairs.

The constancy of color in dominant First World palettes depends on paint chemistry, dye processes, printing technology, and powerful, ever-present cleaning agents (which are often toxic).

This practice of color admits variation with lighting and in the form of artistic intentionality (print, pattern, gradient, tie dye). Colors are often sprayed on evenly, injected and mixed throughout the material, or selected for uniformity. Solid color is the default. Both patterns and prints arrange solidity, usually into crisply defined shapes. But look at the inconstant color of your hand. Technological means, commercial imperatives, cultural norms, and aesthetic practices conspire in First World color.

Any deployment of color, even if it works outside of these conventions, can expect to be surrounded by the dominant First World color system. Red lipstick, white socks, blue collars, striped ties, egg shell business cards, silver watches, and brown cardboard boxes.

Tie dye, color that's faded and cracked, highlighted hair, and vintage fabric emerge as marked dissidents in the regime of color, and to this difference owe their sense of charm and character. That looks so unique!

Because First World colors *abut* other colors, rather than blend into them, they take on distinct identities as things. These things might have never been. Fire engine red. Animals with more specialized eyes do not see more colors so much as more possibilities within and between colors, more shades of red. Even with roughly the same biological capacity for vision, some people can name more colors or are more aware of their associated meanings.

Colors do emerge as things, and these things can be scary, comforting, excessive, connotative, denotative, disgusting, out of fashion, appropriate, or useful. Yet they still function, whether they are things or not, by modifying other colors (bringing out the red in a skin tone), reflecting light, illuminating objects, or affecting that which can see.

Remix

Formally, remix cuts already existing works into useful pieces (e.g. the hook), adds its new contributions (e.g. the beat), and applies its own techniques to both sorts of material to produce a final work.

Formal explanation misses completely what makes remixes good. What makes remixes popular. What makes them fun.

Remixes draw from other songs some of their best qualities. They may heighten those qualities, show them in a new light, or bury them deep within. In this, they identify what those best qualities are. Always something is sacrificed; usually that something is the silence and space between elements. A remix is an improvement, or an attempt at one.

The remix makes the old song about a new style. Ratatat makes hip-hop clean and emotional dance music, sacrificing connection to blues, soul, electro, and everything else that made the original track. (One could perhaps even make the argument that Ratatat whitewashes hip-hop, cutting out the tracks of black music and keeping only commanding black voices.)

Remix is crucial in dance music, where familiar hooks catch people's attention and happening tracks make dancers of them. 'Fever' becomes not just an R&B standard; with Adam Freeland, it's a confident and driving breakbeat track. Most dance music fails for most people most of the time because they can't find a way into it. The track is inscrutable. Techno. Submerged vocals, powerful anthems, and breakdowns all beckon.

Only sometimes is a remix made from a song you've actually heard before. There is a quieter recycling, where songs that were already hits, ones that maybe you have heard but never really noticed, come back to life. Theme songs, club bangers, unreleased tracks, small-time flops, top 40, and forgotten classics are all fair game. Remixes are usually familiar. Mashups are intensely familiar: increase the number of songs sampled and decrease the amount of original sound.

Remixes affirm the possibility of newness in a world where everything has been done before.

Post Apocalypse

Like a snow day, I want the buses to stop running, the radio to go quiet, weeds to overtake the streets, downtown covered in rubble, locals to loot the supermarket, unrepaired apartment buildings to falter without water and power, new social formations in the shell of the old world. I want vacation to come to me. The end of the world.

After the apocalypse, school's out forever. What world is it that ends when the world ends? Somehow, by our desperate and unfailing efforts, we'll be comforted by a cowboy lifestyle at the end of the world. Kill or be killed, just me and the open plains, a time for rugged survivalism and new ways of living. This is transgressive fantasy. Picture me out there with all that old world civilization long gone. This is also an alluring way to feel about myself now.

Consuming post-apocalyptic representation allows we who have homes and jobs, who benefit from the infrastructure the apocalypse would destroy, to vicariously enjoy exposure to an unforgiving landscape, from the comfort of our own homes. A tradition in American literature.

A momentary hesitance about our life commitments, when compared with how we spend our days and years. It lends us a special moment of clarity in which we can perceive 'the world' that might end. The world as infrastructure, order, convenience, safety, ergonomics, purposiveness, and practices. In this moment, the world that would end is not geography or even a whole composed of particularities (everyone you know, every item that exists), but a quality slightly beyond words. It's easy to show, in the duration of a film or story, the scoundrel beauty of apocalypse.

And this is also why it's not the risk of the world actually ending that's so terrible, but the refusal of the world to end (despite unsustainable war, financial meltdown, and endless signs of doom) that performs true tragedy, for its appreciative audience.

Memes Are Just Inside Jokes

Like the selfish gene, a meme is a reproducing bit of culture. That's the idea. iPods, hotdogs wrapped in bacon, driving an SUV.

On the internet, a meme is just a thing people repeat over and over. Retweet, repost, reblog, and share. Calling the Internet the interwebs, captioning photos with the word 'fail,' making fake motivational posters, lolcats.

The theory of memetics is a conceptually vacuous proposition that recurs because it expresses, in the emptiest terms possible, the fact that things happen in the world more than once.

First, memes do not reproduce themselves. Genes can make themselves over again by building the machinery that produces them (although even this requires the conditions and machinery of production be present to begin with). People repeat memes for different reasons in different ways, as groups or individuals.

Second, while genes are sets of chromosomes, there is no thing that a meme is. A meme can be a joke, an image, a format, or a topic.

Third, memetics skips the hard work of understanding why things happen more than once, simply stating that they reproduce. Why do people have iPods? Why are SUVs popular? Memetics says only that such things repeat, not why.

What are called memes on the Internet are really just inside jokes. An inside joke is something a group laughed at once and then continues to repeat. Generally, inside jokes are not funny to anyone else. To use the phrase 'in a good way,' or make jokes about old people at a hockey match can still now evoke a smile, but you had to be there to really get it!

Inside jokes reaffirm the connectedness of a group, repeat a shared reference that makes those in-the-know a group, and reward membership with humor. Inside jokes give a feeling of belonging to people who spend too much time on the Internet.

Inconsiderate Dubstep

Not because anyone else wants to hear it, not because anyone can dance to it, and not because it puts people in a good mood. The appeal of dubstep is that it can hurt you.

Dubstep is louder. Louder songs are more popular than those with a range between the loud and quiet parts. Records used to be made so that a song could build up, peak, and recede at different moments. Today the quiet parts are loud too. A dubstep track simply has more total play time of loud bass, so the loudest parts are almost constant. There's no way to build to a peak except to get quiet first, and after each breakdown comes another bass drop.

Dubstep seem visceral. Of course bass is visceral because we feel it rumble our bodies. But there is another reason. The core of dubstep is bass, and this bass simply *does not play* on ordinary earphones or laptop speakers. Therefore any place playing dubstep is special. It is not just music floating through the air; it is woofers near your head.

Dubstep is dark (like dark techno), omits soft and light moments (there's no singing or peppy mood), and lacks a simple beat for dancing. It prefers sounds we associate with machines to sounds associated with music or people.

Because it's not easy to dance to, dubstep forces a new exploration of movement, requiring new kinds of dance. Though this makes the dance floor less fun, it challenges us to make new movements that will be dance.

Dubstep refuses to offer the comfort of indie rock, the swagger of hip hop, the familiarity of mashup music, or the catchiness of pop. Instead, dubstep's appeal is that it is awesome. It therefore ought to dominate us and it is our place to submit to it.

Learning Not To Kill

So it's a violent video game. Yeah, I wonder too if it it's going to habituate aggression, if it's a way for players to indulge in something naughty, or if it might actually be cathartic.

Video game violence offers something else than excitement, something a bit more unique. The opportunity to control a power that is totally outrageous. To kill a hooker, take the money, and never look back (Grand Theft Auto series). Not just to shoot in a gun range, or with paintballs, but with ridiculously overpowered weapons of the future (First Person Shooters). To run and jump, with infinite endurance, killing creatures that, while able to hurt you, could also be left alone (Mario).

Some games make it a theme: hurting *non-combatants* takes away points! Others make it a point to cause carnage, giving points for needless collateral damage. Most allow more destruction than is necessary, without it influencing the score. What happens sometimes is that the violence gets old. More killing? So boring.

To learn how to handle incredible power is the theme from the X-Men that seems most targeted at pubescent readers: the young mutant has to figure out how to deal. With his bones replaced by metal (Wolverine). With her skin sucking the life from any being it touches (Rogue). With lasers that shoot from his eyes (Cyclops). With the thoughts of others filling her mind (Jean Grey).

It is so easy to kill in most games. Life is so fragile, your powers of destruction so inordinate for the task at hand, for the goals you supposedly have, to the pleasures that you seek in the game.

To kill a prostitute in Grand Theft Auto is excessive and may be twisted, but to speed across town without killing five pedestrians is downright hard.

Reading the Web

Most webpages are covered in text. The margins, tabs, headers, ads, and inset boxes. The body, links, logos, and in the graphics. Readers scan for text. We don't care about images, unless they are big and easy to understand.

Think of it this way: a person views a webpage for less than ten seconds, reading less than twenty words. (Students are not this efficient at reading for school because they don't know what they are looking for or how to navigate academic writing to find it.)

Blazing through pages is a reaction to 'information glut' and a direct result of a design style that has been successful for many websites (especially commercial ones). So it is our behavior and it is a symptom.

People read this way by ignoring things.

Reading a forum? Ignore the dates, user information, signatures, quoted text, situating information at the top of the page, links on the left, ads on the right, and legal information at the bottom. Skip tiny posts, look for long ones. Go too far and backtrack.

Reading an article? Read the title, subheadings, random sets or two or three words near the beginning or ending of paragraphs, entries in a list, the first line of text after a graphic, and the conclusion.

Do we ignore the right things? Do our reading practices make us miss things? Do yours? Because most users for a particular site are regular readers, sites can cover their surfaces with information. Regulars know what to skip.

However, users tend to think that because they are familiar with other websites, they are entitled to skip most of the words on a new page. Readers presume a new page is like all the others. A visit to a new site is probably a temporary mission. In and out as fast as possible.

Sex and Wanting

Sexed identity, central to the political stakes of feminism among other causes, relates not just to self-construction and institutional treatment but also to sex acts. Sex and wanting affect us, and we live them through, imagination, passion, and encounter.

Girl Next Door

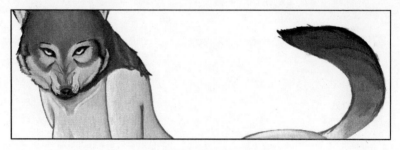

Illustration by Ashley Trinh

They are fractional people. Copies without originals. Only the front stage presentation. A divided individual. The appearance of wholeness that is the ego-ideal. The name of an author without its own authority. A re-animated body.

Celebrities. Artists. 'Household names,' they are people who could instead be cartoon characters or computer models or the product of fashion designers, photographers, lighters, and photo editors.

They exist for entertainment, by the power of entertainment they survive, and in entertainment media they subsist.

What is strange is therefore not that images of women in popular media are so far from what is realistic or normal; what is strange is that these fractional people look like us at all, women or men.

The formula for beautiful women still depends on a sense of familiarity. The girl next door. Why?

The qualities that define beauty are still generated, mostly, by people whose flesh is near to ours. People we talk to, who are real in our real lives—in the limitless openness the word real denotes. Let's go for a walk, there's an 80s band playing in the park. Face to face people are not just images, though they are images too.

They flavor those images. They give those images an association. We can go for a walk together.

People we know define beauty, and fractional people have to live up to their standards, even as the reverse is true (we plain folks try to look like the people on TV). A dialectic of idealization.

Then there are other reasons. The girl next door is a consensus image of beauty, acceptable to many. She is unthreatening and seems cooperative, even subservient. She appears as a relatively innocent regular girl, so it would be crass to reduce her to a sex icon.

Face-to-face interaction keeps these roles around. Robot and aliens, hot or not, don't feel like someone you can come home to, take to a party, or plan a future with. And other looks do elicit such feelings because people play the part often. Affecting a thug style, becoming a punk girl, performing the shtick of inspirational teacher.

A fair question: have we strayed further from the realm of realistic bodies than ever before? Are the fractional people ahead? Phrased this way, it seems clear that amateur porn, cosplay at anime conventions, reality TV, and YouTube videos mark out some kind of territory for the other side (though all of these counterexamples include their own compromises).

Bitch

The bitch is merciless, cunning, cruel, manipulative, and self-serving. The bitch is cowardly, curt, unforgiving, and no fun at all. Violent, improper, and, we secretly suspect, fragile. Less respectable than a badass, more willful than a jerk, less principled than a hardass, more conniving than a boar, less laid back than someone who's merely insensitive.

The bitch is not accommodating.

The word, as a curse word, also has an attitude: to identify a bitch is flagrant, the accusation is too much for innocent ears. In this way, the basic properties of the bitch are regulative norms: ways people are directed to be more cooperative, generous, and calm in situations that do not always make them feel so nice. You step out of line and we'll have to call you a bitch. The pressure is toward gentle and nurturing characteristics that are especially demanded of women. The meaning of bitch is: a perversion of proper feminine traits.

Yet there is more to the word than its primary meaning or basic properties.

Bitching about work. Bitching is complaining. It is to express what is not pleasing, comforting, or useful. A negative and critical mode of action.

The bitch in accounting. Bitch is a nasty word that no one wants to admit they use to describe people they know. Yet we all know bitches who don't act right, who are spineless, or excessive in their manipulative single-mindedness.

Look at me now, bitches! Ending sentences with bitch (or bitches) defines the audience so that the speaker is isolated in a world of unhelpful and inconsiderate others (though this is often used playfully).

I'm his bitch. The name bitch is, like ho, a way to come to terms with how someone is seen or treated, like kiddo, dog or nigga. A reflexive label. It's in this sense that women are casually referred to as bitches; women are bitches to the extent they are routinely treated as bitches.

For some, bitch is a creature inside you who stands up for you, who is not demure or nice or always pretty and kind. The bitch is a guardian angel, one of your many personalities, a bad mood, a survival mechanism, a reservoir for storm water, a return of the repressed. An earth goddess.

The word can do many things, yet when we discuss it outright, we almost always assume it is just a nasty word, an insult. This is not always because we are defensive, but because we do not want to be naive. We don't want to let someone get away with an insult while we take, from their words, a different meaning! Yet, if we always hear in the word an insult, we deny that it is also a powerful mode of action, a technical term for what one is treated as, and a relation to what is supposed to be endured without comment.

No one can change the meaning of a word at will. Explicit discussion of the word bitch can productively monitor its use to secure some combative or less than submissive stances for femininity. But a defensive posture adds to the insult's shock value and ignores its other functions.

Reappropriation won't work. We need to change what the word is understood to mean. What if only women could use the word bitch? How about a story about a lady avenger called simply 'Bitch.' Bitch, Ph.D. Bitch magazine. Affirmations of the other positive meanings of the word bitch.

Body Image: Conditions

Widespread problems with body image are not just psychological, they are a result of cultural understandings of what bodies are, what it is to be attractive, and what people are.

Imagine first a totally different scenario. Imagine we live in a communist society where modernization in a single generation seems possible, where women and men are not just members of society but constitute it completely. We have organized ourselves and we continue to do the hard work, intelligent planning, enlightened dialogue, and everyday sharing that keep us all alive every day and into the foreseeable future. This may be a lie, but if we believe it, women and men make us proud. This makes women and men attractive. They are hard working, well-trained, fair, caring, generous, self-sacrificing; they carry hope for the future of our people. Surely some characteristic will make some more attractive than others: those who resemble our heroes, kind-hearted people from the countryside, those who are strong or do not need to be looked after.

What makes someone attractive in our society? Every attraction will have its many reasons that are local (something specific and unique), but in our memory and planning attraction depends on general principles: smile, laugh at their jokes, bathe. That is, there are some things we can count on and beside that there is serendipity.

Personality is personal preference. Sex seems sexy (although in many actual occasions it is not). The luxury of regular sex with someone you like seems a right, or at least a reasonable expectation.

Sex has become animalistic, linked with the animal biology of pheromones, the difficult to avoid reality of pregnancy and STDs, musculature developed in the gym, sociobiology, and shameful perversions of the unconscious (we can accept that people have them but we still hide them from each other). The role of drinking in the social practices of sexiness should not be overlooked. The word 'hot' has very little meaning but very much function.

You should be attractive to feel good. You cannot count on having a lot in common, magical relationships to fall from the sky like snow, or being appreciated for the kind of person you are. So you should really hit the gym.

Even if this is not your life, it sets a standard for what successful cosmopolitan life feels like, and thereby channels feelings of incompetence and failure. Thin becomes successful, an accomplishment of will.

What does this mean for body image? Attraction implies sex which depends on looks. What is attractive is not contributing to society or working hard at the steel mill, but a cultivated animalistic 'natural' ability to arouse interest. To dress well is good, but the id demands fit flesh.

Sex Sells

The awkward and ever-present comfort of a sex act does not sell. Funny sex, sex that is just too easy to turn down. Lame sex, uninteresting sex, clueless sex. Sex that makes mistakes and sex interrupted. These are not hot enough.

No, we need sexed up sex: sexy sex sells. Sex in the image, graceful sex with line, composition, color, and textures all in concert and balance. Aestheticized sex sells. Sex stylized like the body of Lara Croft, backflips and pistol holsters, skydiving and sly. Bumps pushing through a thin fabric without the obligation and compromise of being any particularly shaped nipple. Sex suggested but forever deferred. Sex so sexy and deferred it can be barely legal and still a virgin forever. Sex so sexy it's illegal on TV.

The sex that sells, the sex that has been sold, has passed through the processes of aestheticization that transform some found thing into a remarkable beauty. Through state of the art commercial photography, through the unprecedented illusionism of Photoshop and compositing software for video (intervening directly at the level of the undeniable real of photorealism), through scripting and directing and telecine and lighting: sex that sells.

All this has fundamentally refigured sexuality, wrought another sexuality apart from a science of sex, with its psychiatry and sexology. This is an eroticization that looks very little like what erotic might have once meant. Exciting, titillating, attention grabbing, interesting, demanding a response, tempting, lurid, seductive, or shocking. But also nubile and available, untainted and inexperienced, skanky and tacky, aggressive and commodified, transgressive and from a much cooler world than the one we live in today.

In becoming the body of a woman, marked by the habit of

being gazed upon, features will be understood and reacted to *in the terms of* this sexualization. The body becoming woman is not understood sexually in terms of bearing children of the race or carrying good sense or a love of God. It is not a body of strength or skill, but it must be flexible and toned enough to make the right marks and pose in provocative positions. It is not a body exuding internal personality, but the surface personality of a loud shirt or car where, just seeing it, it's got a nice personality. Woman becoming the body is many things, but in order to ignite a sexuality it must be erotically appealing on a first encounter.

And this is why actresses and models with 'more realistic' body types do not work and just remind us how shameful and sad it must be to live with such a body. This is why, when a standard for the beauty of women rears its ugly head, its bias is so obdurate.

All this can change, and always has been changing. But not at the level of another woman-body thrown into the image mix: one with no makeup, no digital touchups, or with a body-type Average. These women serve to prove the sincerity of the rule in our living culture: they are really not hot enough to make sex sell. And that's exactly what it comes down to, over and over: hot or not.

Instead, this fashion system of sexuality is where to intervene, at the level of the aesthetic processes and the object-becoming-body-becoming-woman. What objects can arouse the sensations that have come to pass as erotic sexuality? How can women play as images which escape or subvert that lethargic erotic judgment of an under-stimulated audience? Images which care nothing for their hotness are not enough, because it's the audience whose care has executive power. It is with the help of their opinion that we can discover what eroticism can mean besides woman-bodies in a male gaze.

However, the power of this sexualization of women is tempting to overstate. It is stimulating to lazily imagine the constant sexualization of women as the proper focus for our imagination.

Crushes, Beauty

Uninterested, no activity, nothing worth doing—a face in the back of the bus. A pair of shoes in the corner of the room that grow out to legs and a whole instant of persona, look, vivacity. What she's worn today, what particular self she's fashioned out of the elements that, drawn from freshly each day, constitute her self.

He is cute, is he looking at me through those large, dark sunglasses, does he notice me looking at him?

He's just a cliché of homosexuality with his tasteful high quality earphones, ironic and sophisticated shirt, intelligent shoes, truly appropriate socks. How plain his performance of chic cosmopolitan masculinity.

His nose is shaped wrong and his hair quite ordinary.

It is an idle interest, nothing fancy, nothing worth remembering. A familiar gesture, a face that reminds me of a co-worker I met twice and liked, one nice looking outfit, a well curved shadow. It's nothing, really. Or only a bit more than nothing, an embarrassing willingness to like what is nearby because it is nearby. We are quick to forget about it, forgive the imagined chemistry; when everyday life means dramatic exceptions and thousands of experiences as incommensurable as possible, you have to let images go as fast as they come.

Out of the boredom that crushes grow, refining the numb fantasies that they plead with, cultivating an apathy to the failure of these rambling feelings, an unforgiving sense of beauty. Slower than lust and more realistic about its potency, but increasingly narrow in its focus: crushes seek out someone truly good looking.

Why Is Thin Hot?

Why should the body look one way or another at all? Why care? Why do we care?

The usual explanation is that we've been brainwashed by the media to find Angelina Jolie sexy. Then we seek this kind of beauty and confirm it as beauty, perpetuating the cycle. Strangely, almost everyone finds a different beauty in their real life, yet the media keep it up with Eva Longoria and Katy Perry, and we still want that. Like the girl next door, something maintains the cycle on our side.

Why is thin hot?

First, it seems to express self-control. Are we actually attracted to self-control? Are you? People have expressed *wealth* through tasteful garments, but thinness uses the overall look (the body and clothes together) to communicate a *commitment* to keeping your look and possibly your health. We are of course wrong to think this way. Being thin does not demonstrate self-control and self-control does not mean what we want it to mean. Is maniacal obsession, having nothing better to focus on, or being strict and worried, what we want in self-control? Thin is not always healthier, and health is not always thin. Despite this, thin attracts.

Thin looks hot like good design. Thin brings out interesting features, bones and muscles make many subtle cuts and lines. It is architecture. It shows what a complex machine the body is; it shows the body as a complex machine. It feels like an aesthetics that bolsters utility. In this view, the whole body has design and purpose. Arms become functional (lifting, pointing, dancing, gesturing), the internal organs appear more internal (more carefully placed out of the way) when there is less belly, and abdominal muscles show the torso's power to twist and bend. Thin is minimal in size and maximal in baroque detail.

Third, everyone knows thin is right. It's comforting and validating to be with someone thin. It is the right thing to be, and it is rare. You have done a good job. Regardless of who the person is, that they are thin reflects well on you. Although there are dynamics that make this situation arise, the superficial fact of rightness contributes to the situation.

Finally, thin eliminates flab, which we have learned to loathe on ourselves, in the abstract, and on others. Insofar as we believe you must discipline yourself to be thin, our own flab feels guilty and ought to be dealt with (removed).

Abstractly, flab is inefficiency. It is bad design, it is what architecture corrects. It is dead weight, a liability, a freeloader, a sign of age or of being in poor repair. It does not move right; it jiggles and lacks the grace of muscle control with bone support. Fat steals the place of other metaphors, suggesting itself as a way to understand things in terms of how they do not fit or are excessive or unhealthy. This displacement of metaphors is not just a matter of words but of our spatial and kinesthetic thinking.

On others, we see flab as a problem in awkward moments when teachers write on the board, someone's shirt rises higher than it should have, and in the checkout lane where paparazzi photos show celebrity's cancer, DUIs, and heartbreak right next to their cellulite or round bellies.

Associations of health and independence, an imaginary of design, the brute fact of social acceptability, and minimization of flab all make thin hot. The first is a common sense that is wrong, the second is an aesthetics, the third is a social fact, the fourth is a purposivity that people make personal.

Heterosexuality

Do you believe people when they say they aren't gay or straight, they just like people, whether those people are one thing or another?

If a boy kisses a boy, does this make him gay, is this a gay act?

Star Trek's Captain Kirk found his 'best gratification in that creature called woman.' For others, there is no substitute for that one person whom they love. Racial fetish discriminates in a different way. Or, again, cougars, so the stereotype goes, are not just looking for individuals or men, but pretty young men. So, potentially, there is attraction to anyone, only people of a certain kind, or only one person. The obvious romanticization and instability of the third option is what I would like to recover from the others.

In a psychoanalytic perspective that attends to the social construction of the unconscious, individual particularity can be reconciled systematically with 'social forces,' such that her comfort in his strength, and his pleasure in how excited and distracted she is, speak for sexist stereotypes, cultural norms, patriarchy, or commercialized sexuality.

Maturation into heterosexuality depends on the virtualization of desire whose actualization is rather ridiculous. This virtualization can occur through the cultivation of desire for a kind, of which individuals are different specimens (*Playboy* magazine), *or* through the development of a generality that emerges by noticing things in common between many relationships, attractions, pleasures, or experiences (learning what you like). The two processes probably happen together and modify one another. It might be simplest to describe it as a process of universalization from particularity, by whatever means that may occur.

Actualization of heterosexual desire exceeds the central images of heterosexuality. Also important are the detailing of lingerie, the scent of a young man, bras drying on the line, lipstick tubes, long hair, long eyelashes, denim, abs, a kind of laughter, collarbones, cologne, showers. The 'marks of gender' that sometimes fail to report back to a unitary construct of gender.

There are other kinds of purposes to be found through heterosexuality, such as marriage, a real woman, children, or a partner for life. None of these things need to appear through heterosexuality in particular, and the realization of these hetero dreams jeopardize the clarity of heterosexuality, Orgies threaten relationships, raising children threatens the sex life. In this sense, heterosexuality does not even name *a sexuality*, but a kind of absent referent for a discursive preoccupation. Sometimes, the aim of heterosexuality is its own negation, and heterosexuals know this.

These instabilities are substantial, and for this reason, homophobia's work is never done. Ever vigilant, it must detect and handle challenges and contradictions as best it can. But, is homophobic practice a sufficient explanation of the many cases of perseverant heterosexuality pursued by individuals who we would consider accepting, or allies? If it were, then all heterosexuality is homophobic; this would drastically sap the power of the accusation of homophobia. 'You're homophobic!' 'Yes, heterosexuality is always fundamentally homophobic.' (A solution here is the word homohatred, but perhaps a larger problem is in the deployment of phobia as a part of the theoretical machinery.)

Yet, there is a pursuit of heterosexuality despite the instability of pleasure, desire, and attraction that have been articulated through mostly heterosexual means (an aspect of heteronormativity). All I can say at this point is that this dogged pursuit of heterosexuality despite these uncertainties needs to be accounted for, in a manner that makes clear how queer heterosexuality is, without claiming to have thereby effected its undoing.

Marks of Gender

They're not just marks of gender, territorializations of spectacle, nodes in a signifying system of representation. Kitten heels, platforms, stilettos, wedges, slingbacks, and pumps. Or: fur, silk, wool, linen, velvet, suede, cashmere.

Witness not just the *social* but the *passional* construction of real men, whereby we, from time to time, recognize or come into contact with something more than just guys. Passion makes gender by yearning, awe, comfort, intimidation, and respect. And then there is the performative layer: a rhetorical system of regulative fictions in a culture of performance. In this layer, lip gloss is a marker of girliness.

Now, the lip gloss is not just a mark of gender because it is a thing and not a mark. Yet, that it is a thing does not wash the gender out of it. Lip gloss is a treatment of one's own lips, a flavor for kissing, a small thing to buy or give or get. Lip gloss comes out for some occasions and not for others, depending on concerns more particular and varied than one's gender.

This defiance of gender as a marking system describes a wider field of concerns, yet it also marks out another version of what gender does.

Jeans rolled up the calf exceed the usual terms of gender. A feeling of tightness, an exposure of skin, a framing of footwear, a practice of DIY consumerist re-appropriation, a solution for pants that weren't quite the right length. Gendering like painting with colors.

Other trinkets, retaining a strong traction to gender, wildly rewrite the systematics of gender. They creatively imagine a world of more than just girls and boys. Earrings mark out a system of gender that is not capable of self-identity, that depends for its distribution on uniqueness more than repetition, that pertains to several family resemblances but does not chart a dimension for a continuum of expressions, that passes between friends, that we go shopping for, that tends to radiate less diversely through men, that has multiple piercings on the ear.

It's not that earrings don't function in the performance of gender. It's not that projects of understanding gender ought to better attend to those other elements these 'marks' centralize (e.g. the social life of things). It's that gender does not even function as one system, whose divergent marks appear everywhere, whose ever-present performance constitutes systematicity of a single kind.

Gender is not lucky enough to report back to a single (post)feminist imagination because its operations are not ultimately united by reliable translators. Why can't earrings be made to line up with a concept of women useful for opposing employment discrimination? Why can't fertility enunciate a gendering whose position in respect to reproductive rights were more clear?

Each sign carried away on its own path, crossing and meeting only occasionally. A post-signifying semiotic.

If once we wondered why women were in this position, and we then answered that there was a systematic treatment of a gender distinct from, but related to, sex and desire, we are now in the position of having greatest confidence in a kind of magic that rewrites women, position, systematic treatment, sex, desire, and we who bear this legacy.

Playing with Time

Time is not a fundamental aspect of the world. It's just a word we use to describe all the ways it keeps showing up. Time animates processes, locates a present towards which we feel obliged to orient ourselves, organizes inclinations into something called a future, buries the past or keeps it alive, summons the force of centuries, makes us feel up to date, and does much more as well.

Oldness: A New Idea

We have always lived in an information age; we have always relied on networks for communication; we have always used computational systems for the management of large-scale aggregations of human beings, material things, and whatever we want to call information; it is only by focusing almost exclusively on the tools we have in front of us that we can imagine the products we are using today are revolutionary.

David Golumbia, *The Cultural Logic of Computation*, p. 215

In one sense, the explicit output of academic work is the production of new ideas, new theories, methods, findings, and conclusions. Yes, new stuff.

Yet, what is old is a major source of power for academic work. And pride, of course. It has become axiomatic that the creation of newness only happens by the creative appropriation and re-application of things that already existed, as in sampling and remix.

Sometimes scholars argue that our obsession with new things has gone too far. Social scientists dive into contemporary debates to point out that everyone else has forgotten that everything new is deeply connected to what is old. With historical perspective, they then argue that the Internet extends telegraphs, radio was wireless before there was Wi-Fi, YouTube is in some ways like VHS, and images made of pixels are like mosaics. Indeed, the very absence of historical perspective in contemporary debates is telling, they argue. This obsession becomes pathological when we, in our love for what's new, forget what is now old, forget the way 'old' and 'new' function as labels generally, and ignore the connection between what is new and what is old.

So, the argument goes, everyone is too obsessed with things that are new, and should really pay more attention to the past.

I'm reminded of the scene from *The Dark Knight* when an employee at Wayne Enterprises finds evidence that Bruce Wayne is Batman and then announces his plan to extort Bruce for hush money. The employee's superior dissuades him from the plan. The problem, he tells the worker, is that if he's right, then he's wrong. If he is Batman, don't fuck with him.

To diagnose our obsession with newness and offer historical perspective as a corrective is itself a new contribution. A retcon. It freshly re-visions history with sensitivity to the current world (in approximately our current terms). Arguments against newness, in specific contexts, are actually making interventions that are new.

The pose of newness, or its effect, is strategic in discussions that have grown old and which insist that the old is always old and only the new ever new.

Real Time

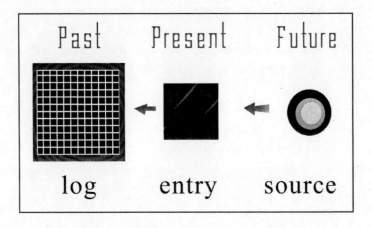

When it's up to date, when it's constantly changing, when it's never a minute behind, when it ticks as the clock tocks, it's real time. This phrase is no longer a colloquial adjective modifying an abstract noun; real time is a technical phrase and its own temporal construct that's going into effect all over.

Real time is data exchange updated sufficiently often that it seems constant. Traffic updates, tweet hits on live search, bus tracking apps, and on-the-fly data processing. They scrape data from a source, tearing it out of context, putting it into a new micro-timeline. The current entry is now, the previous entries get time-stamped and recorded in log files as the past, or are forgotten totally. The future comes from automated data acquisition routines and the data source.

These updates are never continuous. They're a series of states running on underlying cycles so fast that they blur into continuous changing. Flicker fuses. With this blurring together of specific states, real time provides sufficiently superhuman updates that people experience real time at the same continuous pace they experience clock time. More important than overwhelming human sensation, real time can provide functional continuity for systems sensitive to any number of state changes per second. It just has to go a bit too fast for them.

Blur allows real time to appear simultaneous, but the present moment with which real time promises functional simultaneity is only that of real time itself. Lacking real time updates, the present is strictly local. Tying my shoe, fingers passing by, laces twisting and pulled. Real time makes a representation of any present moment interoperable with other real time situations, and this leaves us with the feeling that there is, here and now, a present moment shared by others, which we can keep up with in real time. Yes, real time lets us keep up with it, but then real time also creates that impression of a shared present. And while this technology, in many cases, did not exist ten years ago, the constantly updated present of automated data exchange is now a natural property of the real world, and the most obvious statement about time.

The Ahistorical Past

Splotch of gum on the ground. Marking concrete. Gum blackened by grime, ground in by passing soles.

All around us, the past is present ahistorically. Gum is there, we do not ask what flavor it was or where it came from. However, ongoing consideration of such questions does make an existence that is historical. If we live historically it is because we care about the continued presence of the past and because we understand the past by history, though that history continues (in some sense) today.

To the extent we have ourselves become fully ensconced in lives that are historical, gum's material persistence bears marks of the past, functions as evidence of chemicals in the environment, of weather patterns, of walking, of where people finish gum, and of what they do with it.

There is a creativity to these speculations which they modestly deny. How does one place the gum historically, situate it, invent tales of its past or questions about its present? History as artistic practice.

We do not always live historically. We live in touch with a hermeneutic tradition only more or less. The past exists in the present ahistorically insofar as all its properties are not understood as the culmination or current state (history of the past vs. history of the present) of ongoing events or processes (punctuated vs. continual force fields).

The nature of the ahistorical past is right there in front of us, more obvious than a historical present. It is based purely in reference to objects as they exist now. The floor is a mess. This is actionable knowledge, functional definition, desperate prejudice, or just everyday situated action.

Future

What are the qualities of those things to which we attribute the characteristic of futurity? A futuristic cell phone, a country that makes our own look behind the times, a reassuring image that all will remain familiar and human a thousand years from now (*Star Trek*). Yet, the futuristic is something alien from which we cannot fully extrapolate a world, explicate a mechanism, or respond with any confidence.

The future threatens to destroy the present, replace it, restructure what we understand as here present: into something different. Not always something original, usually there are electronics, lasers, new ways to fly, altered feelings of repression and freedom. Some future is our destiny, but disjunctive possibility describes the futuristic in a way it does not for the historic: there are many contradictory 2020 scenarios and many established facts about the 1920s. At best we can navigate between alternative futures, at worst they will force themselves upon us. In other words, we expect others to face our futuristic as their future, as a threat subject to their choice.

McDonald's is the future, limited data plans, renewable energy, consolidation. Current trends extend or come to an end. Problematics with which we are familiar are worked out in new ways. Often that's how we know it's the future: cold fusion works, computers are intelligent, or genetic discrimination has been institutionalized.

Futurity is not just a name. It is also a feeling. The opening of *Star Wars* denies that it is our future, but we know in some way that it is.

After-Modern

Postmodernity. It comes after modernity, right? If modernity is a period with specific properties that can be found throughout its corpus as practices, ideas, and themes, then postmodernity must be, like modernity, a new age. A new zeitgeist, another way of understanding the world with its own features.

Postmodernism is a style, like modernism, whereas modernity (and postmodernity) is a supposed state of the world.

Authors who write about postmodernity are usually not themselves postmodernists. Those known as postmodernists (such as Jean Baudrillard and scores of lesser known academics) have usually been labeled postmodern by others because the topic of their work is to confront a theoretical tendency associated with modernity, such as an ambition to transparency or a profound respect for knowledge. The easiest way to be labeled as postmodern is to say that a representation of a thing is somehow more important than the thing itself, that such representations are multiple and changing, and that we cannot count on signifiers to mean what they say or say what they mean. This all concerns postmodernism, but what about postmodernity?

If postmodernity were a zeitgeist, it would be similar enough to modernity that it could replace it, at least partially. It would also be only unlike modernity enough that it differed in specific characteristics. With the universal relativist approach, the postmodern is a pure set of variations from an already established list of properties. Modernity plus the prefix post. Alternatively, it is a variation of modernity that might be reduced to a particular case, such as *reflexive* modernity.

Postmodernism does not accept either of these possibilities because modernity and postmodernity are both distinct from the practices that they supposedly describe.

Postmodernist theorists do not accept that we are now is another stage like modernity, that postmodernity exists in binary opposition to modernity, that it is another set of clear facts about the world. For postmodern theory, *postmodernism* is more than a style; it is the material, present, and historically specific reality that is omnipresent and active everywhere. It is the power of threats of terrorism over terrorist acts, the creative chemistry of non-fat butter, and the impossibility of reducing all individuals to any essential identity category.

Defining postmodernity in terms of historical continuity, binary opposition, or a real/ideal distinction would be to adopt the actual terms under critique, or even to capitulate to the terms of modernity, when describing postmodernism. It would be a performative contradiction. (A contradiction between what is said and the act of saying it: to speak 'I am not speaking'). It would be not just conservative, but to miss entirely the point that postmodernism involves shifting ways of engaging with the world, and that that world cannot be regarded in the same way it has been before. Postmodernism is a line of flight from modernism, modernity, and the specific tropes that are the real bread and butter of postmodern critique: presumed correlations between signified and signifier.

Ancient

Stargate, 1994.

A desert on another planet, where a powerful alien keeps thousands of humans in serfdom, is the one place left in the universe where ancient Egyptian language and culture remain. Where the ancient ways persist. Even when it is the 1990s on Earth.

Athens and Rome are not ancient. Ancient India, ancient Egypt, and the ancient civilizations of the Tigres-Euphrates valley were not contemporaries in any sense of time beside this one: they are ancient.

Ancient is not a particular time, but a manner in which time passes. It flows with the patience of eternity, across the ceaseless years of particular human lifespans, in the magical domain that comes before history and reason.

This particular allochrony incarcerates these moments in a temporality so foreign that to even make a comparison between present living conditions and the ancient ones is offensive or at least suspicious. Because we are not timeless, we are historically particular, mobile, and copresent in our contemporaneous real time, living in relativistic times connected by the speed of light.

Anachronism

Something is an anachronism. It is familiar, but out of place. I recognize it, but this is not where it belongs. It is familiar as part of a moment other than the present.

Anachronisms are untimely; they have a strained relation to the present. A carriage on a golf course. A fire extinguisher on a galleon. A baseball cap on a medieval Japanese peasant. A monk on a cell phone.

Anachronisms can be artistic: cowboys wearing Diesel shirts. Also, they can be damaging to historical authenticity: civil war re-enactors with hearing aids.

What anachronistic elements offer is historical connotation. Throw in a stovepipe hat and you get Lincoln, slavery, the Civil War, steam engines, all-wood construction, English accents, an obsession with being civilized, manners, and candles too. This makes anachronisms different from other objects (whether familiar or strange).

An anachronistic hat suggests related objects, a moment in world history, ways of talking and building, technologies, lighting and character types. Like a whole genre distilled into a single drop. With anachronism, we sense the presence of another moment.

Argument Builds and Echoes

Aside from bickering, an argument is a set of reasons supporting a proposition. Arguments are repeated, spread, lose support, allow one to navigate through conversation, respond to the world, and can be refined into very delicate, powerful, fun, or insightful things. Arguments get used.

Ad Hominem

Ad hominem argument attacks the enunciator rather than the content of the argument. It is a type of logical fallacy. The structure of this accusation splits form and content in order to say what is the legitimate domain for debate and what is off limits. Respond to this move by defending the illegitimate or by refusing the distinction.

The author of an argument matters because her position in a network of trust (which is also a community of knowledge) authorizes and qualifies the content of her argument. Conversely, the author of an argument, the being imagined as prior and generative of the argument, also accumulates from the contents of argument. We know Plato by his philosophy, and this often provides (or contributes to) a way of approaching his argument. Similarly, rappers give interviews to clarify their music, presidents give speeches, and works of a particular genre leverage conventions of that genre to help readers get what's good.

With the persona of an author, we can defend against the accusation that a book's cover gives the wrong image of modern surveillance; we can argue that a particular lyricist can use the word bitch, that wolves can kill raccoons, that a social movement can legitimately stir up a little violent riot.

Supported by the arguments themselves, there is a celebrity that corresponds to every author. The dude in a suit at a book signing? He was on Crossfire last night and will be on Oprah the day after tomorrow. He is the one who wrote those words. If we love and respect an argument it directly affects the author of the argument as a celebrity-image and as a device for interpreting the meaning of the text. Publishers and producers certainly hope you get the association between work and author because, among other things, it's a way of marketing the guy as a brand into a steady income earner.

Yet the radiation of argument, the way it may be taken up by others, rephrased, presented in new contexts, permits new hosts for arguments. New authors make old arguments newly. When this happens the celebrity of old authors may follow along, or be brought into play in complex ways. For example, arguing that an old argument was only defensible within the oeuvre of its 'original' author, and cannot sit by itself. Logically, this is a threat without an argument (tell me why I am wrong saying this here and now), but in the mud of recovering arguments from sources and putting them to work, the impression of a fragile transplant can be a significant caution.

Finally, there is the nasty truth that one million customers can't be wrong. They can't be. An author's reputation can permanently change the nature and power of an argument. I mean, what do you think you're going to accomplish defending Hitler's views on vegetarianism?

Why Write

Why write? The cause of an overwhelming habit is rarely clear to those in its grip. Do plants know why they grow, do musicians truly understand why they play? These doers are, however, familiar with their habit enough to muster ample evidence that might be used to establish a reason for what they do. I turn to this evidence to understand why I write.

I would like to write for others and not just for me. There is, for my writing, no seated audience, only scraps of attention like dappled light touching the inner leaves of a tree. The responses to my writing that come from my own reading remain my largest influence; I judge my writing as I read and I write to cater to this evaluation. (This is its own reason to write: humming refrains for myself.)

To me, my writing is best when it is lively and precise, does not overstate or underestimate. When it feels right about what it describes or when it challenges me to change how I feel about what it describes. Would it be enough for me just to scribble, talk, and draw? Something I like especially about writing is that it, like large sculptures and unlike beauty I have seen alone with eyes closed, goes beyond me. In this process, it also challenges me. Creative realization adds something that imagination cannot.

I hope to provoke thought. All writing demands some thought in the process of reading, but sometimes mine asks for a lot and it is rare that a person wants to do this thinking at the moment they happen to be reading my texts. (I do try to encourage them a bit.)

I do think it matters how you talk about things. Yet, I think it is more important what you do than what you say, how you respond to talk than the talk itself. I know I cannot control who uses my work or how.

I do think ideas are aged by poor treatment and, with success, become more a part of the problem than part of the solution. I do not think this is because the ideas were bad at the time. I do not think there is any way to prevent this.

I do think there are more people going to college in the US than ever, and that this gives academic thought entrée to common sense, or more than before. I think some examples of this are obvious: cultural relativism, the idea that gender is performed, and the sensibility (if none of the technicality) of deconstruction. The Israeli army uses Deleuze and Guattari's concept of smooth and striated space for urban warfare, business gurus quote Virilio, union organizers think about Marx. But more importantly, policy makers *presume* Walter Lippmann, cashiers channel specific techniques of math, journalists appeal to justice of particular kinds, programmers implement best practices of design.

The greatest impact of writing is in its echoes. I do not think that citation and quotation are the main indicators of the influence of ideas. I do think that what is acceptable or exciting or backwards is understood to be acceptable, exciting or backwards due to the strength of habit of a logic. Writing can directly engage these habits.

I know the university system is one center for the incubation and refinement of thinking that does its tiny part to preserve or change the world; it changes what the world is and what we know the world must be and what we treat the world as and it does this by thousands of specific operations on things that eventually take as a robust image of the world. Of course, it does this most thoroughly to those closest to it.

Everyone forgets most of what they read. Students in particular. I do think graduate students and professors have a large role in spreading the gospel as well as maintaining the vigor of the theology. I do think new ideas are useful precisely because they are slightly newer, and therefore responsive to the ideas that came before them. It is like fashion.

The reason to write is to produce ideas that might be useful in an environment of other ideas. This is a goal of writing as a craft and a justification for it as an activity

Strawman Argument

You know, a strawman, like what you practice jousting on.

When a text summarizes the argument of another unfairly, and then disproves this partial representation, the text has made a strawman argument. In regular life, rephrasing what someone else is going on about into your own words can be a good chance to show how bad their idea is. Like satire. But it can also be mean, and it might not work if it makes you look like you don't understand their idea or you aren't respecting what they have to say.

But a lot of times, it's a bigger difference that makes a disagreement over something particular. Like how we feel about the term 'illegal immigrant' might depend on some more basic parts of the context where we encounter the term. Often, this is a completely legitimate kind of disagreement, in politics and nonfiction. Hundreds of books just rephrase the arguments of officials and writers into Marxist terms, and then conclude that prisons, eating meat, feminism, schools, top 40 radio, etc. are totally indefensible. This legitimate technique has much in common with a strawman argument.

Arguments respond to something else. They're about things or people or ideas. Only sometimes are they about specific other arguments. The strawman accusation hopes that there is a role for responsible scholarship that can take issues with real arguments made by real people on real issues. Any argument that phrases itself against the surface of a diffuse thematic that cannot be located in a particular text is fighting with shadows.

But it is the varied repetition of arguments, their diffusion and influence as they spill into topics and mouths other than where they started, that make them worth talking about. And this spray of an argument's logic, the reiteration of arguments in different places by different people and with different goals, functions in other arguments as a surface. It must be *condensed* in the moment of forming an argument, so that it can be responded to in its many forms at its many sites.

What does a strawman argument accomplish? It does not claim the surface against which it responds corresponds with a single citation, because an argument is many and rarely just one. It includes a strategy of representation for transforming the argument to which it can respond, which includes a way of reading that argument. It consolidates, organizes, and sets out on its course.

Technological Determinism

How do you make an accusation of technological determinism? Not just that there is more than one technology, but that there is more to be considered than technologies? How do you show that, in a history (of the past, present or future), technologies are doing too much determining? With what meaning of technology do you identify a subject playing too rough with its predicate?

With a strawman. A strategy of reading. Material and mechanical, technique and technical detail become one character: the technology. An account of the technology in relation to some things it's not becomes a story of causation. An account of a (mechanical) cause. Step two, read this account as a denial of other accounts, for its ability to foreclose other rhizomes. Emphasize that, ultimately, the technological account has to be conjoined with other stories.

In this way, the technological, rendered as a mechanical capacity or relationality, can be put in its place. Returned to where it belongs within analytics responsible for maintaining an object for understanding. Objects such as social reality. In this movement's crudest form, mechanisms are properly tools for man, under-stood through social or cultural descriptors. But the accusation of forgetfulness, of an 'impoverished sense of causality,' could also be made from spiritual grounds. The plow did not break the native soil making way for our great nation, God provided for the faithful.

Most often it is social and political realities, cultural change and historical transformations that must not be forgotten. Whole dimensions of forces which dominate the socio-logic imagination like a nightmare. Implicitly, then, these other forces, though they may provide mechanical cause for the happenings of history, are not themselves technological. Just people, you know.

Multiple Words

Pedagogy, medicine, and justice, incite, extract, distribute...

We use multiple words in the spaces of subjects, predicates, verbs, prepositions, or adjectives because our discussion(s) is (are) multiple. It is of many things, responding to many things, open to contingency. Yet we do not say everything at once, do not necessarily include more voices, and we still make an intervention that is particular.

We engage many discussions, many ways of imagining the topic, many vocabularies, to the frustration of perhaps each of them. For it is to each that our lists mark what may be called our disloyalty.

It is confusing and hard to decide which option to take seriously. At my usual reading speed I skip most of the options. Such multiplicity forestalls the making of a clear case, yet the options continue on as a form of knowledge. Hard to remember, useful to quote, good replay value, evasive of rejoinder, less certain, more complex, less comfortable to summarize.

'Deduction' [domination expressed in killing, taking, and demanding] has tended to be no longer the major form of power but merely one element among others, working to incite, reinforce, control, monitor, optimize, and organize the forces under it: a power bent on generating forces, making them grow, and ordering them, rather than one dedicated to impeding them, making them submit, or destroying them.

Michel Foucault, *History of Sexuality: Volume One*, p. 136

Bad Examples

Bad examples can ruin a case, or point to another dynamic.

Good examples reduce a thing to that one aspect an argument needs from it. Needs it to appear as.

Good examples make use of an understanding we already have (or could easily accept) without being able to claim from the example any evidence. The interpretation is baked in: because we already regard everything about Stalinism as bad, it can be used as an example of any negative trait.

Good examples illustrate a point and are part of the form of a particular rhetorical presentation (a speech, a text); examples are not the body of a claim.

Evidence warrants claims. How do examples fit in? Examples cannot serve as warrants for a claim without suggesting a concept, principle, dynamic, mechanism, or texture that exceeds the example (that is more general than an actual event). They cannot be evidence because they don't represent anything more than themselves (they are anecdotal). They are not a claim, or the example would itself have made the claim entirely by itself. The example may have already made something like the claim, but in a different context or in a more obscure way.

Bad examples introduce uncertainty, confusion, and doubt. You say everyone is angry about it, but your example is of a person who is always angry, or is exaggerating for the camera. Is this anger the current form of anger that is ongoing? Is this anger intensified by opportunities to be heard?

The bad example is more than lacking. It's suggestive. It points another direction, adds a twist to the moral it is being asked to stand for, confuses what we thought was being discussed with something else that maybe we should be talking about instead, pushes the audience back out of the grasp of persuasion into the crossroads of apathy and doubt.

Personal Taste As Method

The official position is that all opinions are as varied as they are inexplicable as they are unimportant. Different strokes for different folks. Everyone's entitled to their own opinion.

This is a practical outlook for executives. It's what the marketing report says, so no one would be offended if you followed its recommendations. Movie studios and TV networks cannot count on your opinion. They experience opinions as quantities, because audiences are primarily sales and ratings. In this sense, *Avatar* and *Titanic* are the best movies ever.

Likewise, those with *no* investment at all in what other people like would rather not make waves about what a movie is about, what a song means, or what strange interpretation you come to from your own fucked up life.

Suits and randoms agree, the meaning of a text is not important.

Yet there are those who care what they think. Their idiosyncratic interpretations, their own preferences, their personal taste somehow ought to be considered by others. Is it because they are arrogant? Or, is it that they are parasitic, trying to make their own art (and paycheck) by trashing other people's hard work?

Personal taste is a key method for cultural critique and social commentary. It works not because the author is unique or a towering genius. It works because we're all living in the same world and no one is that original. It works because no impression or reaction is totally singular, even those that are perverse or fleeting.

It works because, in reading a book, one is not just an I, but also a we, experiencing as the selves they might have been. Were I Jewish, a navy man, someone besides myself. To the extent there are reserve materials, untapped potentials, or a social *prior* to the individual (and not *just* the result of it), personal tastes are communicable because they come from the community an individual would communicate with. However, this idea goes too far when it posits fully formed and well distributed values and opinions across a seething mass of strange people. 'Culture is shared meanings and values.'

A critic is not just connected naturally to how others feel; one must become attuned to how others see and react. From this, a critic gains access to what is thought but has never been said, has never been heard, has never been recognized in what others say.

For the education of a critic, the idea is that if you know all the conditions beforehand (culture, traditions, precedents, values and opinions), then you have a good idea how something new will play out in those conditions. This is a challenge to understand beyond sweeping generalizations about culture; the critic must understand or intuit the more obscure bits too. How malicious is an octopus. Why fashion made femininity modern. Against these fragments that we don't yet know what to do with, we have developed less immunity, are less sure how to defend ourselves. We will deny these less readily; they can feel true longer.

In the formulation of private taste into communicable opinion, critics turn shared or resonant feelings into arguments or attitudes that can be taken up and repeated by others.

Empiricism

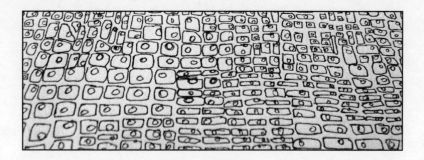

It's the sun, finally back and warming my face. It's global warming, it's weather patterns, it's all in my horoscope, it's going to put him in a better mood today, it's a reason to go outside, it's yellow light, it's the way the world will end, it's an excellent source of Vitamin D.

Empirical thinking is not just a preoccupation with particularities, details, materials and things. It doesn't mean you just notice more things. It's a continued interest in things as examples, as beings insofar as they may be becoming-evidence. Not as facts, motives, niceties, unexplainable singularities, background, or parts of a body that is mine.

Empiricism 'reduces' things to their evidentiary function. Reduction in the sense of focusing, rather than eliminating. Empiricism attends to things as participants in the construction of a theoretical summation. That summation may be a long standing project, modified by the new measurement, or still unformed. It may be stodgy or inventive, reflective or unthinking.

Mediums Representing Things

We hope to make a representation of the original that is also different from the original. A drawing, for example, rather than a face of flesh. But the part that is different creeps into the original and has a character and potential all its own. Beyond the use for which it was summoned from the netherworld, the representation wanders on, appropriated for a moment but far from dead.

Evidence of Glass

I know that I can see through glass. I know that it is transparent. I know that that transparency has a materiality and character. I find that character placid, familiar, and clean.

Windows don't only remediate views or art. They are not a substitute for a mountain vista or a landscape painting. They are a kind of wall, or break in the wall, whose visual impression on us is not an image. The visual impression of reflectiveness, glare, shine, a slight warbling in older glass, a tint, a bit of dust or dried rainwater. Evidence of glass.

There is a particular way glass lets things be seen, and this distortion, coloring, or clearness has a materiality of its own.

Scale

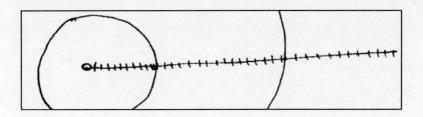

From a distance, it was nothing at all, not even a speck. Closer, it not only took on shape, but became many parts, joined in particular ways. (The observer can enter into its complexity, not just know that it's complicated.)

When it was small, I could not see that I would interact with something so slight. For snails and insects, that meant I might crush them. In scalable polygon count objects in a 3D world, that meant they need not be rendered, and perhaps need not even be made to exist. Forks and pieces of sushi cease to exist as the ball becomes large in the Katamari games.

When something is too small or too large, we become numb to it. Perhaps unable to detect it, perhaps unable to affect it. Tinier than my measuring tape's smallest marking, it eventually stops counting as any quantity at all.

This numbness does not foreclose all interaction. The sharks could not bite James's giant peach; they couldn't open their mouths wide enough. At different scales, different things can happen to each other.

Scale is extension/reduction or movement negotiating commensurability. The negotiation, that is scale. As scale changes, different things change at different speeds. Five miles over the speed limit is minor at 80, but huge at 10. Scale changes, changing the segmentation of each input's sensitivity. (How a tree feels global warming is not how it feels carbon dioxide or warmth.)

Faces

Faces are distributed institutionally and on social media. More people see your face now than might have a hundred years ago. Machines have amplified our faces.

What a face does. A face communicates and looks back at us as we sit with someone or even as we pass by strangers. Now the face is most often a flat, stationary image (how often a jpg?), photographed from whatever angle usually by someone (usually younger than you?) who waved a camera in front of your face and took a picture that turned out ok.

Why faces? For most people, the face is a unique identifier. It's rarely covered and near eye level. Since the mid 1990s, an image of your face can be stored on a computer and relayed over networks with ease.

We allowed ourselves to be treated as faces. People accept the face as a primary marker of identity. To have many people know your face is to be famous. We believe faces are unique to individuals and show their personality, unlike bodies which are evaluated in other terms (too short, too blocky). We know our own faces well from mirrors and our own photo albums and we accept them as our signature, as a sign with an authentic connection to the self that one is.

Collecting faces. Because we can recognize someone easily by a face (partly because we've been socialized to tell the difference between them?), using faces as markers of identity accentuates social behavior. Humans respond socially to faces, regard the assemblage of data the face represents as a person. This is harder to do with a user name or thumbprint. When we see a face, it seems aware of us; we respond to it as if it might respond back. The face has become an important part of who someone is. Because people accept their face being used, because technologies support it, and because the way people respond to faces is useful, the identity of a person now has an authentic existence in an image of his or her face. Not voice, not name, not signature. Face.

Totalization

What is 'always' or 'only' commits us not to never encountering exceptions, but to a way of attending to things by which our commitment can be honored. All gamers play to win, to the extent they are gamers at all. There are no definitive counterexamples for unshakable faith.

If the first person plural arrogantly takes on the role of representing what it cannot always stand for, at least it can be strategic in revealing an aspect of that collective it totalizes without totally knowing.

If all objects are fundamentally *temporal*, eyebrows, birdsong, ice cream, and mountains take on a temporal aspect. The future, past, and rhythms of eyebrows, all very important. Rapt attention.

Totalization is not total. It's an incomplete and ongoing process of universalization from particularity.

Network Diagrams

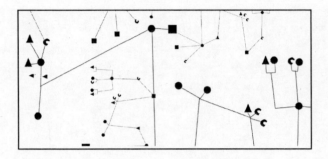

Network diagrams show lines connecting nodes. Big nodes, square nodes, thin lines, or dashed lines. How do simple diagrams represent complexity?

The nodes are either in a geographic position (spatial) or positioned to make the diagram easier to read (aspatial). Varied node icons (e.g. shapes) or parameters (e.g. size) allow a few versions of a default node, but these variations inherit properties of the default node unless inheritance is denied specifically. They are all basically nodes in a network.

Likewise for lines, connection is understood as presumably the same, though sometimes a bit different. Differences are permitted; different ones must be translated into differences to appear.

These diagrams omit many things: the context of nodes, content of connections, active sites where connections join nodes (how input puts in), parts of the assemblage without connections (these are simply not included because they don't connect), materiality of nodes or connections (bodies or mediums), role of non-connective substances (dirt around the roots), and work involved in animating the traffic that the diagram maps (coal powers computers, people drive cars).

These diagrams are important to describe how others have thought and planned, in which case we can appreciate what's ignored or edited out. The diagram can be insightful.

However, the formal properties of this diagram emphasize formal qualities that, while discernible in almost any system, may misdirect us in a regular way. Everything seems decentralized, redundantly connected, shared, up-to-date, information-based, semi-autonomous, and heterogeneous yet comparable.

Internet activity (diagrammed as data links) can be about art and community; airlines' routes and flight times vary with weather; there are many lines of responsibility within a bureaucracy despite a clear hierarchy; rhizome growth depends on nutrients and soil conditions.

Typical

I am typical. And this typification multiplies the power of my action. I spend most of the day sitting at a chair, I like to eat salty snacks, I have a mobile phone, use my debit card often, ignore things that seem distant and unimportant, don't like war but do little to stop it, try to save money, like good music, forget to dust the living room.

The power (social or political) of being typical is not the agency of my free will. In being typical, I do not stand alone. I am not unlike the others. I am not out to have my voice heard. I am not the agency of my opinions. The power of being typical is exactly the power that lies in my apparent passivity. In my easy-to-ignore humdrum banality. Like dharma or Tao, it appears bland or conservative, but is also active and infinitely intricate. Paradoxical and incomprehensible, the typical is not hard to summarize. It is too easy to summarize.

Norms and demographics represent what is typical. They will often order and stand in for the typical. They supplant the typical. True, but this portrayal is like saying that a window is a barrier that keeps out the cold. It is also representing something. It is a surprisingly effective creature at letting us know, in its strange way, what is on the other side of it from the viewer.

It is the typical that norms aim to discover, and shape. It is the typical with which government programs, the work of art, and corporate consultants must negotiate. It is the typical that we accomplish in our least individualistic moments, although our most vain attempts to be unique may amount to the same thing as well.

The typical has been known by other names, such as ideology and cultural politics. These also organize the humdrum of everyday life into a mixed form of action and meaning, held together by repetition, truth effects, and hegemonic deployment. But the typical is also accessible to me in everyday life in another way than observation and analysis. I can back into it. I can express the power of those who appreciate graffiti by turning a blind eye to its creation. I express the weakness of the DMCA by getting music for free online. I embody the rain's strong suggestion that I not go outside.

I am a point of contact between political projects, cultural change, the weather's power, and my everyday life. I am an artic-ulation, insofar as I am typical. I do the work of making immanent translations of transcendent tendencies: I am a focus group.

Normal

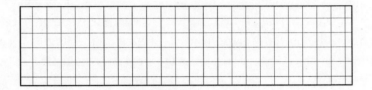

That is not normal. Everything else is normal. Like a normal day. A normal person. A normal piece of pizza, a normal movie, a normal idea.

But what is a normal day or a normal movie? Normal is a horizon (vague, exterior, without distinct limit) that conditions our attention to the particular. It is a way to compare actual things to general and vague criteria. Considering the normal, anything can appear abnormal.

Yet some attempt to move things toward the norm. The normative is that which carries moral force, tends to be true, is well enforced, or is a desired goal. Normalization sorts the irrepressible variety of the world through an apparatus of discrimination to create a flow that can be more easily integrated into designated functions. Normalized mp3s, normative time, statistical convergence to the norm.

Does this normalization go too far, extend the norm too broadly, and trample difference with the imperialist hubris of monoculture? Or is the vision of a smooth, unflinching, 'basically' undifferentiated surface that is normal paranoid?

The normal is not a conspiracy, organized, understandable, and directed by intent. It is a thicket of the misunderstood, strained, and out of place. A normal Iowa boy on Mars, a normal jet engine in your bedroom, a webcam used for normal portraiture. There is only normal relative to what is strange, the contrast by which the horizon of normality appears shifts, and all that which has been normalized appears again as strange.

Destruction

A bullet does not negate every fiber of your being, but it does end your life, thereby constituting a complete biographical subject who didn't exist before, and is more integrated and coherent than ever. A piercing weapon, a slashing weapon, or a blunt one. None need vaporize an entire body to destroy. Each must do just enough to be destructive (a threshold of destruction). Touch the wing of a moth, shoot the zombie in the head, put a stake through the heart of a vampire, rain on a parade.

The destruction is of humans and property. Not flames shooting out into the air. Not seagulls scorched by the sound miles away. Not pictures taken of smoke and terror. What can be destroyed is our sense of security, our comfort, our community, but the violently manic patriotism thereby produced cannot be destroyed by a blast.

Destruction is an effect that makes a system retroactively of whatever becomes, in destruction, a structure broken. It disrupts flows, rather than takes lives. It is phrased negatively, though its function is also positive. In some cases, we do know destruction by a positive term: deforestation.

To destroy infrastructure starves the people, ruins their power lines, smashes the roads, saps the bridges, prevents trains from running on schedule, fells grid structures, and reterritorializes the smooth flows of water, power, and transport with broken construction materials. It does not temporarily obstruct, but undoes the integrity of what composes the structure. Denies functionality even if the roads were cleared and river restored to its original state tomorrow.

That which now exists is not the same as that which might in the future be said to have existed after becoming destroyed. You never know what you've got until it's gone. The city becomes the proper whole by which the broken parts will not be known; destroy a thing to create a medium, the thing, by which its parts will be known. It was a keystone species; it was true love.

Destruction's creativity is not just retrospective, for it is also by destruction that ground is cleared for grasses to grow. That we realize dependencies and connections beyond our previous understanding and that new patterns of growth can take place where before they had no success.

Things You Can't Really Know

You don't completely know but you've still got to act as if you do. If this is what everyone has always been doing, then this is one sense of what it means to know. Yet it is a way of knowing that dreams of something beyond what can be seen or reasonably believed.

Intelligence

Don't deny that you find some people smarter than others. You already treat them that way. Right now you could list off ten people who are smart and five people who just aren't.

Unfortunately, the idea of intelligence has gotten a very strong moral association so that to say someone is smart or stupid is to make a kind of penetrating judgment of character. So we call people stupid as an insult and forget what the word means, because we can never speak openly about who is dumb, only who is smart.

One reason intelligence-based insults remain popular is that so many other tempting negative descriptors have been banished from polite speech. It's not acceptable to insult someone by suggesting they are gay or foreign, but it is ok to suggest they are stupid when you really mean they are wrong.

Some people are smart. This does not mean anything about performance on formal intelligence tests. To say someone else is intelligent is to make a judgment; the judgment makes the characteristic real.

It is an evaluation we make based on the small challenges, tests, and opportunities delivered to a person in the normal course of life. We see intelligence performed. Or it's an opinion we form based on what we hear and how we see particular events go down. 'Seems like Jim's being a moron again.'

William Burroughs said that intelligence is 'the ability to adapt oneself to new situations and environments and solve problems, obviously a useful instrument that will probably be laid aside eventually.' Still, we value intelligence. Is stupid always bad?

The abstraction of intelligence has no naked form; it can never be seen in a pure state, because we don't really know what problem someone is trying to solve (a feint, a change of plans, a misguided intention), because familiarity, knowledge, and skill can substitute for the adaptability of intelligence, and because it's rare we can agree on what a situation or environment *really is*.

Because intelligence is important to us we have many words for it, many concepts of it. To be intelligent may mean that one is sagacious, clever, witty, wise, well-read, quick, able, enlightened, sharp, keen, resourceful, thinking, profound, smart, original, talented, savvy, with-it, or brilliant. There is a wide range of meanings here, and while some engineers strive to create artificial intelligence, we still do not understand the artifice of intelligence.

Miraculation

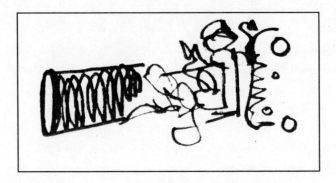

Dark windows, shoe laces, concrete floors, a small tree. Birds, a plastic bag, brown sludge, cigarette butts. The ahistorical past.

Things exist. We do not know where they came from. In what sense can we even say they came from somewhere?

Things emerge from other things. That is what we know. (Or, when it is what we know, it is how we know: shoes from factories.)

Is it the process of production that creates something that comes out? Is there a mechanism to causality, a mechanism that can be seen by what it does in excess of what it needs to do to produce?

Though there may be machines, explanations, bodies, forces, light touches, and tiny, gentle factors that contribute, they are secondary. What is primary is that a thing emerges from another thing, as if by a miracle.

We not only know that chocolate comes out of a package but we act as if this is true. When we add to this account, we know that it comes out of a shop where it comes from a factory where it comes out of a machine where it comes from chocolate that went in that came out of a refining machine, perhaps, or from some

152

other place. But this does not always erode our conviction and expectation that something called chocolate will emerge out of the package.

When we see Wonka's chocolate machines, as when we discuss who is smart about their work or what parts of a computer are working properly, we are explaining the miracle further. We are expanding the miracle: what are the machines, how do they work, what do they come from? The miracle does not disappear, it is just accepted calmly.

Just as the imagination feigns a personal identity from the bundle of perceptions we take for a self, so the miracle fictions a collective identity that brings with it its own normality and rationality. The miracle is perhaps an exception to the constituted order of habit, but it is just as much, and more interestingly, the inception of a new reality. We must take Deleuze's enigmatic and felicitous remark on the miracle seriously: 'To believe in miracles is a false belief, but it is also a true miracle.' The true miracle is collective fantasy as a real social actor. Let us supplement Deleuze with an equally felicitous remark by a commentator on the Deleuze/Hume relation, Jeffrey Bell: 'For Hume, the more a belief is constructed ... the more autonomous and true the reality of that which is believed.' Said differently, a belief that traffics among wide ensembles of groups as though of its own accord earns a kind of power of truth that can reshape the very way the given is given. It becomes a quasi-cause, coupling itself with every facet of social existence (and so quasi-causality, too, is a matter of 'constant conjunction'), yet claiming the mantle of the unengendered: by playing the part of the presupposition or precondition of all experience, the indispensable key to a specific distribution of sensibility, the miracle miraculates. Though it may begin its career as 'mere' fiction, it becomes the only true reality.

Kyle McGee, 'Machining Fantasy' pp. 849-950

Imagination + Creativity

Imagination is both wild in its absence of recognizable system-aticity (his body sang like aluminum foil, all men on earth died instantly, dreams parading through each place put me to pasture), and domesticating in its terrible repetition of the same (dragons, robots, the four elements, travel back in time but disturb nothing, machines have taken over, heroism, and true love).

Imagination is not just a set or a faculty. Imagination is not just a personal trait (that daydreamer...) or the inventory of fantasy (D&D's *Monster Manual*). Imagination mixes the available with the possible, it permutes thematics into possibilities. All the athletic shoes that could be made, every racist thing someone might say about Ethiopia, what would be conceivable to make for dinner. Some imaginations are explicit about their limits: Waffle House lets you have your hash browns scattered, smothered, covered, chunked, topped, diced, peppered and/or capped. When you can 'get your burger 256 ways' it means eight choices and you get as many or few as you like, same for the hash browns.

Yet, so often, we hope that imagination is, in its fashion, the author of creativity. That its prefiguration of possibility determines practices of realization. That it is its own virtualization whose legacy will be clear by its actualizations.

Imagination isn't just the author restated as a diffuse social force. But we do often defer to the authority of an imagination and insist on creativity as the realization of imagination.

As a person is hosted in a human body and can thereby reproduce by means of bodies, imagination's need for proliferation depends on its reproduction through creativity.

Creativity, unlike imagination, need not be thematic or consistent with itself. But because it's wild like that, it's treated as the ground, the host, the tool of imagination. This organization of actor and agency does not dominate creativity or obscure crucial social processes, but does let imagination take credit for creativity. And does participate in the telling of stories where imagination is the main character and creativity is the chaos with which it deals.

First, creativity does not just mean material affordances (film budgets and crews), but also tends toward empiricism as a method of inventivity (Michel Gondry's homey props), and is the locus of much vivid artistry for which imagination must account. Creativity is creative and not just productive.

Second, audiences do experience imaginatively, which is why we may want to treat imagination as expressing itself through realization (the artistic vision brought to life by the hands of a master). But audiences, are not just experiencing imaginatively, they are also audiences acting creatively.

Creativity and imagination are different but do really well together.

The Oracular Mode

...once we stop using theory as a declamatory tool, once we put aside an oracular mode of analysis, once we understand that, even within capitalist social relations, diversity of experience is not some kind of mirage or unfulfilled yearning. There is a lot to do.

John May and Nigel Thrift, *TimeSpace: Geographies of Temporality* p.36

Theory is a summation of the best available knowledge into ideas that can be applied to make sense of things. It is a denial that serendipity is more important than control. Theory represents things, compresses information, and limits our attentiveness. In exchange, it lets us perceive in a new way or on a new scale. May and Thrift name this tendency correctly, and here I would like to make a case for this aspect of the theoretical. Theorycraft is very much like augury, clairvoyance, or magical insight. It is an attempt to know beyond what is knowable.

What, if anything, demands theory? Why have theory at all? Theory is not necessary; it results from accumulation and organization, which happen often even in chaos. Theory forms because it is wanted. There exist desires for answers, tools, predictions, wisdom, and techniques (systems). Often these desires are impossible. We want to see patterns in the unpredictable; we want to know the purpose of a group when, objectively, none exists. These are desires for the transcendental, divine, and mystical.

A simple oracle: magic source mediated by a priestly interpreter tells visitor divine knowledge. A contemporary form of this is daily horoscopes. Part of secularism as a cultural condition is that we don't believe gods speak *through* priests; we see the channeling priest as a talking human. Like the Wizard of Oz, there is just an ordinary man behind the curtain. If this is our cynicism, it demands that all insight come from sites where we believe agency exists. A man, the unconscious, a conspiracy, a cultural habit, a technology. These have agency, the spirit world does not.

The veracity of the secular oracular mode does not come from the source so much as the mediating methods of interpretation. Statistics, how experiments are designed, reflexive ethnography. That is to say, we trust the priests to foretell the future because we can rationally discuss how they arrive at their conclusion. We do not bother trusting what inspires them (a movie, a crashing wave, a phrase in an unrelated book); any mystical guidance they think they got is officially *their* shit.

The methods of interpretation can be made quite explicit and, it seems, can therefore be taught. We accept that academics, lawyers, and policy analysts have nothing to hide. However, productive work of this kind cannot always be taught. It requires a character and situation that must be selected for, involves doing work that is implicit, and students ultimately must discovery for themselves things that cannot be explained to them. It's critical that methods appear teachable because this establishes secular credibility, and strengthens the claim to rationality. Super-fancy rationality.

Theory doesn't work because of easily explained methods. A theory works because it resonates with an existing situation and gives to us a perspective that is an orientation for action and perception, for plans and responsibilities. Foucault on prisons. Butler on gender.

Economic policy is the same way: imagine how things will go if an institution changes its policies.

Theory is clairvoyant because it tells us where things will be and what to expect. We can see what is not visible, because the oracular mode assures us of its location and nature. Freudian approaches look for repression; Latour anticipates relations between taken-for-granted objects.

We who are deeply engrossed in a theoretical approach (be it Marxism or method acting) will appreciate those who let it guide their actions. We can understand what options are available to them and which options are chosen. Their noble reliance on the explicitly rational but implicitly mystical guidance of theory becomes heroic, or at least more interesting because more familiar.

Theory is augury because it tells us how events will transpire, even when we know the future is unpredictable. It can be hard to establish that a theory is wrong because theories are less directly connected to outcomes and because they tend to guide how we evaluate outcomes to begin with. However, when a theory is wrong, most people will regret the choice to take the oracle's advice and either try to go without or find another oracle.

Practical Reflections on My Death

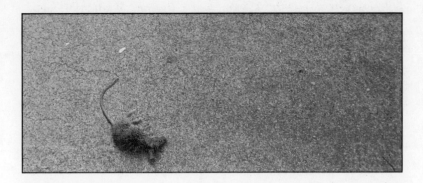

When I know how long I have left to live, then I can know what it is I will do in my life.

I know already the approximate date of my death. 2060 or sooner. It's the opposite of an expiration date, because there is no guarantee and there are no preservatives. Although the cause of one's death always comes from outside, we are born to die, and death frequently punctuates my life. A little bit of me dies. That night something about me changed. The one you know who did those things has gone and can never come back. For those deaths no one mourns. Often we're happy to see such death in others. With that part of you dying, you've improved. You quit that job, lost those friends, stopped hoping for something, stopped hating some part of the world.

The tragedy of death is that it portrays a totality that was me and announces that it has past, in its entirety. Death is surprising because we don't interact with whole persons of the kind death renders. In life, one matters to others only in fractions. Death creates a totality that it declares dead, which everyone then must read back into each case of the one who has died. The case of his finances, the case of his forgotten friends, of his secret misdeeds, unspoiled leftovers, and of his remains.

These all become parts of him.

When I die my name will not be deleted from all databases; it will, in most cases I think, be added to my record that I am dead. My organs may move to new hosts. One hopes to die without passing on debts, but passing on is what death is: the dispersal of matter, the transfer of control from one to others, the movement of some self that had never before existed out and away from all that we know.

Pictures of me will not be impacted in any serious way. That which I have will be disposed of as my relatives and friends see fit. I, as a project developing along the course of my life, will be in their hands. That I has long been something I promised ('I will never lie to you,' or 'I will have my revenge'). It has also been claimed as my property for description ('that's not what I meant,' 'you don't understand what I was doing'). This I will require other animations, which will, as bodies inevitably do, fail too, in time.

When I die I will no longer enjoy the burden of accounting for myself, I will become more virtual than events and become voiceless. I will not see, hear, touch, smell, or taste anymore, even if forms of experience do follow the experiences of life. In some ways, I will break from the inertia of everything that ever happened to me. Insofar as I am incorporeal.

Some very sad people will have to clean up my room and throw away my stuff and sell what they can and I hope that from all of that someone else gets my speakers and sharpies and eats the snacks I kept. But I also have, in the consideration of practical confrontation with my own death, a calm sense of ethics with a less vivid sense of cause and usefulness: please throw away my bad art and old magazines. Ironically, the books and furniture that were only props to my performances might be useful to someone else, and even make them think of me.

Should you think of me again? I hope to be shaken off like a dream whose lingering makes the day hard to begin. This feeling may be impossible to bear when living, as it is life that insists on living. But, in death, I feel sure, thinking of me will matter to me not at all. Think of those other things, and do what you will with my remains with the confidence that you have more of me now than I do. That you have had this much of that substance I call me for a long time already.

A Grain of Sand

To see the world in a grain of sand,
and to see heaven in a wild flower,
hold infinity in the palm of your hands,
and eternity in an hour.
William Blake

To see, in the slightest gesture of another, a world of desolation, betrayal, hopelessness, and a sense of purpose so embittered it denies any longing for better? Why would anyone put that shit on the fridge? Would holding infinity in the palm of your hands be so rosy? How many eternities are in an hour of suffering, desperation, and fear?

Accessing another dimension, on your own like Alice through the looking glass. Why would this be uplifting and sweet? First, there seems to be one account of who we are and what we are doing. I am driving to go shopping for packing tape and light bulbs. In practice, we have to deal with a few versions of most stories. I am part of a consumerist culture driving a polluting car to exchange my wage for trinkets I will soon throw away. I am a stand up guy for getting this done right when it's needed. The traffic lights are doing their best to slow me down.

These animate different world-frames, but navigating the

differences between such visions is a habit for us. So they feel similar by virtue of our regular exercise of their commensurability.

We are subjects, if that relation might be descriptive in this case, of a few imaginations. And against this feeling of being totally incorporated into one story you might not even like, you might want to see heaven in a wild flower. The appeal of this image is that we are so dominated by the same stories, that a rogue fantasy heroically presents the possibility of something else. It does not have to help us break away from our condition in the dominant fantasy. It gets us with new terms, forgetting what came before. Is the new fantasy better? The standards seem to be pretty low, since we're amateurs in the new imagination, still surprised we can fly. We don't spend much time in it, and have a superficial relation to everything there. Better than vacations, there are no expectations, so there are no disappointments. Better than changing what you get up and do every day, there are no stakes, so you can't lose anything there.

Visions of reality are not something we have to believe. One of our most powerful resources against them is ignorance. Not understanding why we are members of a global community that requires us to maximize our own utility can be a powerful means to frustrate and defy that logic. Social sciences that study how actors choose make the opposite assumption: only by understanding your position can you hope to have any power in changing your place in it. Many argue that it doesn't matter what you think, as long as you participate in the system (whatever the system is), this will come to be as their vision of your reality compels others to acknowledge and follow it. When its echoes resonate and amplify its compelling dominance.

Some argue that by paying taxes you are a slave. Do you feel like a slave? It's surprising how persuasive it can be when someone tells you that it doesn't matter what you think because they are sure. It drives us toward the good life of microbes living on a grain of sand.

Plateaus of Style

We draw from the reservoirs of what has been done before, appropriate from these styles for our own actions, and thereby stabilize the diffuse and personal experiences of reality into transpersonal styles. These styles become known as they grow in popularity over the years, but it is always up to an individual to pull off the style, to make the style work.

Parkour

Parkour. Scribbling all over mundane masterpieces. Works of construction and architecture whose targets are first that world for which the human body is the measure of all things and second that world of architecture photography of clean lines broken by trees and benches, shot in summer.

The rail was to prevent children from falling, to discourage the wild ones from taking risks at the edge, for liability reasons, to catch those who slip near the edge, for ADA compliance. The rail was a prefabricated design they had painted black to look like a silhouette in the sunlight.

Athletic, acrobatic, energetic, young people, whose bones and bodies can still withstand the blows, who have trained for years at gymnastics, martial arts, dance, or for strength. They will make themselves an exception. The untapped potential of the training they have received, in a tradition they may have left behind, will blossom freshly in parkour. These people will climb and jump, run and grab and pull and chase and turn and hop and leap and stabilize themselves. And fall to the ground and get up and try this spot again a few times next week.

A staircase just wide enough for three average bodies abreast. A ledge just high enough to you look down from it, but too high to sit on safely. A wall wide enough for two strangers to sit back to back.

Traceurs are not whole, everyday people. They tend to be 14 to 26 and male, with a background in something else that they make relevant here, each in their own style. They tend to meet up for more interesting practice in groups, but exercise and train alone during the week. When they do this, when they use the techniques which they understand to more efficiently allow them to get from point A to point B, when they jump down the stairs, landing in a roll, when they swing and hang and make a precision landing on a pipe, they are traceurs.

Traceurs will make themselves an exception to that institutional reality of humanism that orients itself not to the spirit, but to the individual, flexible, particular, material human bodies which are primarily distributed around an average, yet also include a few legally protected outliers.

Parkour finds the most direct route from any arbitrary point to another: point A to B. Not from the patio to the bathroom during lunch, or from the grass to the parking lot when the park closes. Practice doesn't focus on particular points, but techniques for increasing the efficiency with which types of obstacles may be overcome. Ways to straighten lines that often don't have any other reason to be drawn.

We tend to walk in predictable, curved, wide paths which can be cropped or cut or turned or angled by the provision of paths. We tend to walk and talk and sit and stop and lean, see, lie, bend, and turn in sufficiently normal ways, all of which can be understood and responded to with wood, asphalt, steel, plastic, drywall, glass to manage the freedom of bodies in space.

Traceurs are not ignoring the rules written into the built

environment, they are putting the measurements to completely different use. A 6 foot drop, 12 stairs, rail to rail, a long cat crawl, a good spot to practice a technique. The basis of their practice is bodily motion that diverges, that climbs instead of keeping its distance, that leaps across instead of walking between.

Smart

Something is smart because it reflects our own reactions and makes us aware of them. British comedy is preoccupied with proper behavior, with decorum, and with thinking that goes astray.

It is not smart because of its outcomes. We laugh at all kinds of things: resemblances, the offensive, shit that's ridiculous. Something is smart because it seems to go about things in the right way, to such an extent that exceptions and accidents prove that there is something systematic from which they depart.

Smart. Now that's how it should be done.

What is smart primarily sounds smart; school and corporate culture reward this. It is different from brilliance, intelligence, wisdom, cunning, cleverness, being sharp or bright, experience, and resourcefulness. It is different from getting the job done.

Something that may happen simultaneous with smartness is the invention of a logic that feels like it was already our own. Sometimes it only sounded like it was going on the right track because it had that rational sound to it, because I wanted to believe it was basically saying what I was already thinking.

Counterculture Politics

Counter to the culture of America, there is the counterculture. Historically we're talking about a bunch of burger eating college-age kids pissing off their steak eating parents. We can't worry about the legions of uninspiring participants in historically important movements, since most Panthers were probably pretty respectable citizens after all. The 'hopeful' understanding of counterculture is that it had a political impact on the country: we got more liberal because of them. They made it ok to be a minority or a woman, and emphasized what a privilege it is to be a white man. So we're talking about civil liberties. Freedoms to privacy, requirements of tolerance, inducements to guilt. Counterculture, then, is a political thing. It has ambitions and strategy, so we can say it was more or less effective, or that we are forgetting what it was supposed to be: free speech protests, anti-war activism, voter registration, bringing the rich more in line with everyone else.

In this interpretation, counter culture, implicitly of the 1960s, has become the new Founding Fathers; we should do some real deep thinking to figure out what they were really saying and how they really meant for America to go. So counterculture was not a temporary and stylish expression of political passion, it is a living platform, a definitive political agenda, and we are charged with its execution, by any means necessary (democratic politics and being anti-consumerist and recycling). It's a strategic mistake to take someone's involvement in politics as an indication that they really are going to care and stick with you forever, but it's also like trying to keep dating someone while pretending you haven't already been dumped.

Hip has not *become* a marketing ploy; hip and cool have always survived in relation to commercialization and will never be destroyed by real cool looking ad campaigns (unlike the politics). Imagine if young people wore bell-bottoms and dug psychedelic rock for some inscrutable reason other than their unity with a political agenda fixated on fair trade. Maybe because protests were cool, radicalism sounded fresh, and something was in the air.

Martin Luther King became an action hero, an action figure. Another celebrity, icon, face to stamp on everything, and a character to connect with you in the marketing campaign for your cause. Art does not belong to politics and become sadly co-opted by commercial use. Style is a rogue trader, using politics and products, used by them, and hardly about to settle down and marry any of its many collaborators.

Counterculture has no set relation to politics, and the vision it expresses most often does not map onto the political spectrum at all. Gaming, unassociated with any romantic plans for live music to accompany the revolution, developed directly out of the computer's interface and have their own take on reality. In gaming, the world is not created once but again and by competing companies, takes place at all kinds of scales, and can be interacted with in circumscribed, but very powerful ways.

Will we remember gaming as a vision of a better world?

Emo Comfort

Alienation, as if it were alienating to recall the horrible fit between the world that confronts us and how we like things to go.

Groundhog Day. Awakening every morning in the same terrible world provokes Phil to drinking, suicide, even learning to play the piano. He is alone in repeating this day, and all the universal throb of humanity in which he finds himself again and again only reminds him that this is not where he belongs. Until he discovers that this day belongs to him as it does to no one else who lives it.

Donnie Darko. Aware that the world will end soon but not in any position to change or improve anything, he has just his private fantasy: our soundtrack, his hallucinations, the things his lame hypnotist does not want to come across, the things his insipid gym teacher can't understand with her self-help paradigm authored by a fraud.

The secrets of our hidden pain, in emo, are open secrets not worth trying to explain to those who don't understand, not worth trying to talk over with mom. And also not worth getting over, because they're our relaxation, our community, our trademark.

Fantasy Aesthetics

The imagination is a musty old cellar. Odd things fill it: dragons, goblins, things that made you cry as a child, nostalgic scenes, and tired-out clichés.

Fantasy art takes that imagination and sets the rules in opposition: a castle is boring, and many things are made of glass. But, now, imagine a castle made of glass. New questions arise. How does sound travel through it, what is visible and what is murky, how could anyone keep it clean?

Fantasy implicitly valorizes a conservative playground world of white perfection. Beautiful maidens, strong and good noble men, thrifty and hardworking poor people who are never bitter, petty, or deceptive—even the evil are thorough and well-organized. Do these represent audience preferences, safer ground for publishers, a development from storybooks and fables, or simply a topic that is culturally associated with fantasy? I don't know.

In any case, the valorization is implicit. It is not the explicit content and is rarely the main attraction. Fantasy is boring when

173

it is only strong men struggling against evil monsters. What is really interesting is the weapons, armor, tide of battle, magic conditions of unrequited love, and architecture of the castles in which all this courtly romance transpires.

What fantasy aesthetics foregrounds are the extreme rarities. Not just a dragon that hasn't been seen for decades, but the beast itself, fighting a battle and, for the first time ever, losing.

Socialist realism, in comparison, focuses on ordinary scenes (or, images presented as if they were ordinary): workers in a foundry, a bridge built, officials talking to peasants. Fashion photography shows the exceptionally beautiful in ideal photographic conditions (conditions ideal to photography generally), but presents it as tiny moments of the ordinary life of those who consumers long to be.

The convention of fantasy aesthetics is to mute the complicated connotations of an image. Busty women, orcs who are animalistic Africans, magicians who stand in for the educated elite. These are not 'problematic representations,' the way they would be anywhere else. Because the content is explicitly not a part of the real world, it presumes to have a special license not to care, not to make socially responsible representations.

For some, that license means fantasy can deliver a world of pleasures, undisturbed by the realities of inequality, diaspora, or other issues of social impact.

However, what fantasy aesthetics also offer is to invigorate the imagination by breaking its brittle forms against each other, and leaving this mess to the viewer's creativity, which can recover from the strange results only by a stretch of the imagination. By creative reception. If it does this for castles, trees that walk, and gnomes, it should also do this for black animalism, oriental femininity, and the goodness of white legalism.

Mixed Mode: 1980-2020

For a long time there has been photo collage, film montage, mixed-mode art, multimedia performance: creative appropriation and recombination for entertainment. This is not specifically contemporary, though it has gone through major changes recently.

The essence of 80s postmodern pastiche washed up on the shores of Europe in the form of Hip Hop acts, repackaged to summarize black, urban America to other countries, starting with Bambaataa and others in 1982 and culminating in Digital Underground (where Tupac got his start).

In this early stage of postmodern style, the performance was to intentionally disrespect and disobey by selling out, doing things wrong, going too far. There was a feeling that the world was all quite wrong (whether because of the communists or the anti-communists) and a maniacal joy ride was one's only hope for personal salvation.

In the 90s, disaffection got organized, picked up the name Generation X, and produced grunge and globetrotting hipsters who were politically active and tried to be smart too. Wearing a Che shirt meant you listened to Rage Against the Machine, and probably had some thoughts on sweatshops, globalization, and global warming.

The 90s collage began to make bricolage tasteful, sometimes by bringing it to a common language, so the pieces interacted in a nice way. However, when people talked about the style, it was still imagined as an exercise in tackiness. Any random thing coupled with any other thing. As if the fact of mixture was itself the entire appeal.

Only in the 00s did remixes become tasteful products on their own, rather than novelty goods. With Napster (dead in 2001, started in 1999), the number of remixes people listened to exploded, and even though most of them were just one more inane 'techno remix,' this moment introduced a new idea to many people—that a remix might be better than the original, or at least pretty decent on its own.

The tasteful remix has now gone too far, and the decoration of bags from Trader Joe's show mashup as mainstream. Convergence ideologues expressed the essence of this lame idea: soon everything will be digital and it will be on one device. This makes mashup lose its distinctiveness and also begins to make everything that's sampled seem like a mashup of samples itself: the Grey Album. The cliché that has now won the title of 'hipster' wears tight black clothing, ironic sweaters or facial hair, and feels stupid and alone without the company of those who get all their inside jokes. They feel elite because they believe that most people don't understand them, which is actually very much like the self-isolating melancholy of emo. Why do hipsters love bacon? They eat what they like.

For most of the 80s there was already a sense that social responsibility should be a part of art, and that the illusionism of presentation should connect with community and ordinary people. These themes were extremely important in the 90s; Eminem and Jewel were *authentic*.

Throughout the 90s, we hoped for remixes that were not just dance remixes where the monotonous trance beat wholly overpowered some sampled pop song. The same would be nice in movies. In the 00s we got this new breed in spades. Mashup and remix flourished, films aggressively transcend genre boundaries, prints dropped anywhere on any shirt (or pants or vests or jackets) are an ideal medium for inserting other periods into the present.

What we now have wanted for a decade already is stylized mashup, mixed mode with personality, montage with strict rules. *Pirates of the Caribbean* actually came pretty close. In action films, we want fighters who can do various tricks (parkour, flips, shooting, kung fu) in a combination that is specific to them. MMA is still growing in popularity; it's already surpassed golf and soccer, by some measures.

In clothing, we want period costume that is made today. Steampunk, for example. In art, we want to see when the artist is appropriating something from somewhere else, and use that in a way that fits the track, while still producing a song that is original overall, especially in atmosphere and soundscape rather than just in sound bites. We are already producing this.

Sagacity Teaches Wisdom

The inarticulable is the habitat of wisdom. In the realm of the unsaid, in regular contact with that which exceeds the imagination, living among things done which can only be spoken of as memories.

It does not come from experience or reflection alone. At times, sagacity teaches wisdom. In this case, what is the mechanism by which a lesson is learned? Teacher gives explicit guidance for well-named possibilities, but the truth of the name of a concept cannot be understood without particularities which can find verification in the student's own examples.

Lessons:

- You treat people you know now as characters from your past.
- 'To the extent that metaphor can be thought of as a language of desire and as a means to recover what is absent, it is essentially anti-poetic.'
- 'To pretend, I actually do the thing: I have therefore only pretended to pretend.'
- 'Never resist a sentence you like, in which language takes its own pleasure and in which, after having abused it for so long, you are stupefied by its innocence.'

A full example for a concept cannot be provided because a proper and compelling interpretation of each element and relation in the case must already inhere in it, which would require the example, in fact, be the principle which it would demonstrate. Effectively, learning wisdom requires the transformation of one's own sense of how to understand an example so that the example demonstrates the particular principle. This cannot be forced.

Imagine pretending to do something, recognize that you have just done some thing, and now deny that you have pretended to pretend to do some thing. You have in fact done it, and only you believe that you merely pretended. Or, you have in fact done one thing, which shows that your act was only a gesture at a serious attempt at pretending. Or, perhaps, both are wrong, but realizing that these are wrong requires the thought that visits wisdom.

In this way, being smart may help the student imagine illustrative examples. However, this quality may also encourage the student to distort the principle, or find other ones … and not all principles are equal.

A significant variation between different practices of imparting wisdom is the degree of confidence the practice has in representation. Some lessons mean what they say, but in others it is the meaning of the terms, the interpretation of language, or the voice of the lesson that the student must come to a new understanding of. Zen koans are an extreme case.

Sagacity tutors thinking that has not yet found comfortable expression. Wisdom does not make arguments or put feeling into words. It re-orders feelings and thinking in a way that makes a difference both when put into words and in the semi-lucid living of your life.

Selling and Buying Things

We see ourselves and each other with all the terms that have ever been used to describe a person, but, to the economy, we are rarely anything more than consumers or employees. The universal trade of capitalism makes us hybrid as technology makes us cyborg. How, then, does demand come into being?

Excess of Dreams

Capitalism demands an excess of dreams. It crushes dreams, provokes others; it finds a use for dreams that are healthy as well as those that are dying.

Perhaps we are naturally over-productive of dreams. Then capitalism puts those dreams to use. A dream is something to work for, and is therefore also a reason that can be given for work that takes places. Dreams retrospectively account for what you are doing with your life.

The American Dream gives hope or comfort or an excuse. There is not, in the end, any way to tell whether it has been achieved. Yes a white picket fence, but the garage is falling apart. How much is enough? What was it that you really wanted anyway?

Becoming wildly famous is a dream we're interested in, although few are actually interested in working for it; we're game for watching celebrity, contemplating it, smiling at its happy parts, and feeling torn apart by bad parts. We pay for pop music about pop stars, reality TV about people as random as those that populate our everyday world who can become famous, tabloids of celebrity gossip, and video games that tell the same stories of legendary heroes.

The dreams you choose *not* to pursue are dreams we enjoy in entertainment, and entertainment can be found in almost every consumer product. The dreams you choose, are they dreams of success, accomplishment, confidence, comfort, splendor, nobility, and kindness of the very best kind? These dreams can be put to work, and capitalism is the economic system that will put them to use.

Money Feelings

People care about money. Of course, we all care about things that money could buy or that we do just for the money. But we also care about money itself. It is, to us, more than a bare intermediary whose only quality is exchange value and the funny looking presidents on the bills. In addition to standing in for values, money is a thing, a substance, a style of representation. Like evidence of glass or the austere sincerity of print journalism, it is not just form and content but a thing.

Money is gritty and tactile. In affective registers, we fetishize it in just the opposite of the usual Marxist sense. Marxist commodity fetishism describes the regularized understanding of things as exchangeable objects, the reduction of craftsmanship and historical particularity to potential exchange value. Selling something on eBay, we present it as a thing that is worth money, usually stripping it of any unsightly backstory about where it came from and what we did with it.

We fetishize money in the sense that money itself gives us feelings, commands attention, interacts with us through other intermediaries.

When we imagine money, we feel bitterly its slipping away, long for its embrace, and fear its sinister excess. For some of us, it's best not think of it at all. That's the promise of a full-time job with good pay and solid benefits, using debit cards, having an accountant, or Forrest Gump investing in Apple. Fiscal stoicism. Does it not elicit feelings in you to see someone get paid, throw away a dollar bill, or blow $500 on a nicer exhaust system?

Money is a medium whose material forms (cash, numbers on a screen, quantities spoken or calculated) we feel strongly about. Money can feel like ambition: cash money millionaires. Money can feel like corruption and soullessness: addicted to money. Money can feel like an everyday struggle: the paper chase. Money can feel like subjugation and misery: bills, debts, and poverty.

Green

Environmentalism sees a beautiful natural world that finds itself threatened constantly by the activities of the human species. Odes to wild beauty are political expressions of this environmentalism.

Hiking, camping, wild animal parks, ecotourism, landscape painting, nature photography, the promise of REI equipment, and HDTV specials such as *Planet Earth* attest to the diverse beauty that is at risk in questions of environmental impact.

Simultaneously, a language of resources, production, tons, hectares, infrastructure, trade, and net margins informs policy analysts and regulatory bodies.

One environmentalism is of majesty and reverence, wherein we must preserve nature out of respect. The other environmentalism calls for efficient management of resources produced by nonhuman processes.

The first approach fails insofar as we are bad at being reverent. We have lost the habit of obedience to majesty; grandeur does not win fealty. The second approach sunders because the numbers out of alignment are never really one's own problem: water is still affordable in Southern California, the expansion of deserts in Africa doesn't dent my bank account, and no one nation can stop global warming or regulate oil consumption down to zero.

However, these approaches have done something. The first has given many people a positive motivation to act. The second, while unpersuasive to ordinary people, has given regulators terms and justifications to pressure large organizations (governments and companies). This pressure has yielded results.

Together, these two have turned environmentalism and ecology into something trendy. Being green.

That a product, practice, or policy can be called Green makes it attractive to decisions makers. Politicians want more green stuff on their record, businesses want something green to appease regulators and improve their public image. Regular people want things to be green because it feels like the future, might be more healthy, provides the moral satisfaction of goodness, and makes the future hopeful.

Green means very little. Organic, recyclable, low carbon emissions, less pollution, less toxic, more efficiently produced, grass-fed, green in color, compact in size, sleek in profile, adorned with an eco logo, associated with deciduous trees. Any one of these will do.

Yet the enthusiasm for all things green has worked. It has motivated purchasing decisions, has encouraged new social practices, has supported hybrid cars, recycling, biodegradable plastics, emissions regulations, media coverage of pollution, and increased sales of organic, herbal, and recycled products.

The hype has made the difference that neither preexisting crusade was able to make on its own.

'Brand' as Brand

Establish a consistent deliverable with a specific character. Make every instance of it point directly to a symbol epitomizing the brand identity. This will establish a known and desirable identity that attracts consumer action (spending). Do it for whatever. Airlines, restaurant chains, apparel, cars, cities, office supplies.

This is the brand formula. It works because it relieves consumers of the need to trust competitors (skip local diners, pull over for McDonald's). It works because it promises quality and character across a diverse range of products (Nike).

Branding's apparent effectiveness is also a consequence of business practices that have already created the outcomes the marketing department will claim credit for. Kitchenless restaurants, well-researched franchise locations, an already established consumer base, economies of scale, stronger coffee than anyone else, vertical integration, first-mover advantage, better partners in the supply chain, anti-competitive pricing. These practices may establish a strong business, and then brand can be added on top of it all.

What if the concept of brand has itself become a brand? Each thing identified with the symbol of Brands seems thereby instilled with all the special power of advertising to make us do what we do not want, of marketing to know our habits better than we do, and of contemporary business sense to accomplish the feats of our modern world. The corporate weirding way.

Any thing said to work as a brand (DJs, local newspapers, a reputation for good barbecues) thereby promises to be more reliable, of a known quality, and attractive to its potential audience. Brand may work for strangers consuming your product. Or the idea that you've got a brand may work to persuade others that you've got a dependable attraction going.

Brand can be made to describe any activity.

Whether its end is fame, art, love, or money, the goal becomes interchangeable with a successfulness understood in economic terms. Teenage girls getting MySpace friends or YouTube views are, the one making analysis in the terms of brand will argue, basically making a successful business.

In all the famous cases, brands miraculate attention and success. It is as if Goodyear got rich simply because it was a brand, by the power of brand alone. Branded goods are often cheap, mass produced, and superficial in their appeal. Is Burger King impressive as restaurant, cuisine, or dining experience?

Appropriating branding as a strategy presumes the autonomous functional effectiveness of brand identity. But it remains a (difficult to answer) question to what degree branding, as a business practice, contributes to success (measured by profit, business growth, or otherwise). If brands succeed because of work done around the company and not simply because of the matching fonts and colors, then to say something works like a brand indicates only a resemblance to a consequence of economic success, not necessarily to an engine of it.

What does brand really do? To imagine this, it might help to imagine a company with no brand. Its style copied by imitators, its pronouncements written in all fonts, its graphics drawn in all styles, with any colors. Internally varied, externally inter-mingled, inconsistent and indistinct. What is lost? What is gained? Does this happen?

Why does it not? Is it for profit, for efficiency, or for quite different reasons such as the handwriting of the person who makes the signs, or inks available at the store in that city?

Brand, as a consistent deliverable and generic symbol, is comfortable. It is easier to accept than to question and compare, and so we will pull over for the decent services we know it provides rather than go elsewhere.

The Drug Paradigm

If it's caffeine, it's a drug. Whether you drink liquid extracts from plant matter that contains caffeine, chew caffeinated gum, or down pills of the stuff, it has the same effect.

As injection, suppository, smoke, food, or topical rub a drug enters the body and has an effect. What effect?

Drugs get you high. They alter the state of the body, they impact experience; they are therefore discernable. But you can't always tell what's going on, or that something is going on at all. All day long every day, the state of the body is changing. There is so much in flux: hormones, blood sugar levels, concentrations of neurotransmitters, moods, feelings, thoughts, activities, respiration, heartbeat, age, allergies, the cultures of microflora that outnumber human cells in your body ten to one.

Drugs are compounds (or whole plant parts) described by a pharmaceutical model that has a basis in organic chemistry, molecular biology, and neurological study. Quality exists only as expressed in the combination of active ingredients present in a dose. MDMA, LSD, diazepam and ethanol are specific chemicals. These are active ingredients that are ingested with inactive substances. Excipients in pills do have function; they color, flavor, bind, preserve, change dissolution rates, or prevent active ingredients from sticking together too much. We nevertheless consider them not drugs, and hopeless enthusiasm in the US still prefers 'pure molly' (MDMA in a gel cap) to more carefully put together tablets of ecstasy.

(Marijuana includes many active ingredients, and is thus a problem for the pharmaceutical understanding of drugs. The reigning pharmaceutical solution is to focus attention on THC, despite the existence of hundreds of other active ingredients in the plant that vary its effects. Some drugs are specifically taken as cocktails, such as Ayahuasca and lethal injection.)

The pharmaceutical approach works pretty well for figuring out what to take, what someone has taken, and what might be helpful in making a specific alteration of a body's state. It also means we are all drug users. Which drugs when, that is the question.

The word 'drug' is the generic noun form that can be occupied by a thing that we have a well-developed way of not-understanding. Three things can be known well: dose can be measured, a known chemical can be detected, and possible effects have been studied with categorical and qualitative approaches. Two things can be known vaguely: an individual's body and its experience under the influence of the drug.

The rest has been ignored. Mood, situation, state of the body and what it hosts, mode of intake, time of day. Ignored are those more difficult to explain (culturally and personally specific) and more intimate demons that make marijuana something beside a simple soporific factor inducing appetite and impairing short term memory.

The paradigm invoked by the word 'drug' is that any case of a human body intaking a similar drug is basically comparable to any other. In this way it is like an incomplete version of nutrition science, focused forever on antioxidants and calories, hesitant to lose its scientific basis by considering a bigger picture.

Life is Good

Do what you like, like what you do. (The slogan of the Life is Good brand. I just got a shirt for xmas.) Is this a command or a description of how people actually live? For economists, a person's likes and habits are the same. What you do is what you like, what you like is 'really' expressed by what you do. The really pitiable specimen is that actor who has not been reconciled with its identity as chooser. The person who spends money on what she doesn't like, who likes things she isn't coming any closer to getting.

Often hopeful anti-capitalists try to say people aren't *really* rational, so economics has got it wrong and we are really free and The Man is lying. Part of this is to use psychological evidence to say that human behavior is not really *hedonistic*, and therefore the psychological model implicit in economics is not true. But the criterion for truth is totally different in the two cases. In the anti-capitalist argument, truth is irrefutable description of enduring conditions. In economics, truth is empirical, and units of this empiricism are the identity of chooser and choices made, which are automatically reconciled at a theoretical level that isn't susceptible to empirical challenge. A person chooses what they like because that's what their likes mean. This is a useful empirical unit for economics, and no one cares if useful units are tautological. A centimeter is a hundredth of a meter.

But the mistake economics make is to ask for us to become self-actualized actors capable of standing by our rational choices. Do what you like, don't waste your money doing things you don't like! Spend money on things that help you realize projects as a chooser, don't spend it on things that are not important to you! More importantly, like what you do! If you can like your pathetic excuse for a life more, then you, the thing that feels, can be reconciled with you, the chooser, and the thing that feels can get the increasing levels of prosperity to which the modern world entitles it.

So I'm adding to my shirt, just beneath the big 'Life is Good' logo a stencil of an authoritative white guy on an old fashioned TV, from whom the words will then have come. Life is officially good, you stupid mutherfuckers.

The Persistence of Power

It is by our actions, all of us, that we make conditions that make some things harder or easier. By what specific mechanisms? By the ideology whose excuses we mistake as our own life story, the hegemony of some alliances over others, by the material empowerment afforded by consumer choice, by the dominant agenda?

Common Sense

Common sense. You know, that thing that smart people usually don't have? You know, that thing that the commoners still believe in? Old wives tales, just plain talk, urban myths, just-so stories, what every man knows in his heart, the consensus that bias would wrongly distort.

Here is an argument that has become popular: common sense is worse than wrong. It is a protective sheath between our aware humanity and the part we play in hegemony, it is an everyday form of ideology. We need to get beyond common sense.

Let's be polemical. Common sense isn't one thing, there are many common senses, as well as uncommon and rare ones. Let sleeping dogs lie. That thing about seven generations. Don't mix business and pleasure. Between them, there is almost always a dispute, a contradiction, or a completely different perspective.

TV dinners are a convenient meal that lets you relax and watch your show. Just as much common sense as the critique that a sedentary lifestyle is unhealthy, as critics concerned that we have a body image out of proportion to our actual lives, as those seriously trying to scare us that American children are dying of epidemic obesity. There are plenty of obvious things to say that are not the same.

There is no central authority of common sense, no founding fathers, no primary texts, and no schools of interpretation. Logics that seem common circulate through people who will live and die by them at one time, and laugh them out of the room at another time. Organizations don't just take actions, make rules, or maintain systems, but also think, and that means engaging opinions, and that means accepting some kinds of sense as reasonable and some as not worth discussing.

Common sense is not just a rationalization of hegemony, though, for being that, it's also a survival mechanism. It is more than a strategy or a mechanism, because, like capitalism, it is more than useful. Common sense is a purposing machine that cannot be understood only in terms of accomplishing goals, because it also sets goals, it also inspires purposes, it also moves us.

The vulgar language of common sense is not a simplification or pidgin of the kind of proper academic prose that's kept alive by highbrow intellectuals and writers. It's the thickened, congealed, boiled down, necessity and opportunity of the everyday becoming of language out of things that are said over time by a wild 'community' of speakers. It is a history of folks who've had a go with it, and all the things they've had to say and the ways they've gone to put things better.

Academic thinking, academic language, like proper English. Common sense thinking, everyday talk, like not grammatical or nothing. The vulgar is molasses, it goes between implication and clarity, even at the moment that it seems the most plain way you can figure on to say a thing. Because the thing to say itself is ambiguous, and not just because it has been articulated all fucked. It's not one thing and it's not the enemy.

Rules | System | Intelligence

A rule is a conditional statement, by which an event is defined and responded to in a set way.

There is no incest prohibition; instead, there are sequences of incest that connect with sequences of prohibition following specific coordinates.

Gilles Deleuze and Felix Guattari, *A Thousand Plateaus*. p. 176

A system is an arrangement of rules whose enforcement, contradictions, and propagation follow organizational logics. Systems include rules.

Subjects are simultaneously bound in enmity and dependency, a contradiction smoothed ideologically by economic theories of the hidden hand, political theories of the benefits of interest group conflict, and philosophies of utilitarianism, each of which converts competitive self-interest into the common good.

Wendy Brown, *Power Without Logic Without Marx*. p. 84

An intelligence entails a manner of considering, deciding, rulemaking, and executing that presides over a system, but also makes possible its transformation, recuperation from failure, response to exceptions, and approach to things unknown.

The value which an actor surrenders for another value can

never be greater, for the subject himself under the actual circumstances of the moment, than that for which it is given.

Georg Simmel, *On Exchange*. p. 52

The point is not to phrase things so that you can always explain everything, but to be able to keep together a few ways of putting things by which we can negotiate with things we understand poorly.

Claims

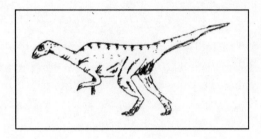

The film made some strong claims about identity.

This is the gateway to ideological critique. What has transpired is rife with claims, definitive statements which are advocated and behind which the thing itself can be understood to stand, in support. An interactive surface of claims, wherein we can locate the actual position of a work of art.

Vicissitudes of intention, duplicity, expectation, outcome, expediency, character, affect, and voice line up in a claim. Claims follow from warrants, which, themselves, assemble evidence. But claims are not only the end of this logical chain, they open outward to argument, strategy, chatting, discourse, and boredom.

In the diagram of ideological critique, all movies and games, texts and art can be assessed. Identify claims. Remember that the thing is on the other side of the claims, that they unstoppably issue forth from that thing itself. Abduct those claims into a political discourse. Make the thing answer for what it's said. Don't stay quiet about it; you are contesting its cultural work in a material manner by performing your critique. So stick with it!

First there is the claim, then there is a spatiality of position-ality, then a discourse into which claims can be entered. In the first stages is the objectivity of a modest witness. With translation of claims into a discourse (which is also a political terrain), lines of flight transform this objectivity into the modest heroism of an everyday activist. An oppositional reader.

Ideological Aspect

Usually we understand ideology with reference to political tendencies and voluntary participation in a system that does not benefit you. It has become popular to avoid this language because it seems to treat people as 'dupes,' a very strange insult almost never used in normal conversation.

The basic dilemma is this:

Don't TV ads tell us terrible and insane things all the time? Yes.

Does anyone ever truly believe them? Never.

Are we influenced by them nonetheless? Those who say yes, and are interested in pursuing the point, are interested in cultural studies.

Perhaps, though, the ideological can be decoupled from the political.

The ideological is an aspect of language, it stems from claims. That is, every claim is ideological insofar as it projects a world, universalizes things and contexts. Text from the trailer for *Road to Perdition*: 'Every Family has a Destiny,' 'Every Son Holds the Future for His Father,' 'Every Father is a Hero to his Son.' Slogans with profound truth only in the context of this one Tom Hanks movie. Yet the words do not specify a context, that is something we infer for ourselves, without being aware that we do it. The claims have a worlding function; they provide a horizon beyond which we can expect landscapes as great as what we can see now.

This universalization happens in each case by the performance of description (performative denotation), which is a minimalist performance (a cool medium in McLuhan's sense) that competent audiences understand. This understanding transpires through creative use of the imagination: 'We Sell Boxes and

Moving Supplies' must be made into an image by each of us. William Burroughs explains that language can give words, but it can also put images in the mind. The devilishly polite can use all the right words, while drawing terrible pictures in our minds, particularly images that put us in lowly roles.

The ideological is a function of language wherein it functions by worlding claims. How we respond to those claims remains open, influenced strongly by traditions of interpretation but still susceptible to unexpected and unruly other ways of understanding. The strategy of oppositional reading clarifies and consolidates the ideological aspect, articulating it to political realities to produce the outcome of a 'political' stance. (The stance is political because it involves reference to political realities.) It makes a reductive interpretation of the ideological aspect of a thing, and responds to that abstraction.

Identification

I watch gangsta flicks and root for the bad guy
turn it off before it ends because the bad guy dies
50 Cent

Sometimes I'm watching a movie and realize that I hate the main character, definitely. And whatever bad things might happen to this character, bring them on. Especially likely in horror movies.

Not in all cases is identification a procedure securing a self that is mine, although appropriation and belonging are important terms in its function. Identifying can also be a kind of empathy or sympathy, sensitivity, solidarity, or means of evaluation. Identifying with a police officer shows the difficulty and banality of violation and enforcement of 'the law.'

Identification gives you a new perspective: the *Grand Theft Auto* games show me a stereotype of who I am, what kind of car I drive, and what music I listen to—but they also show me how to navigate a city during an outrageous high speed chase.

Identification can strike you but without guiding you: I want good things to happen for Chameleon Street, but that doesn't always mean I want to act like him.

Identification may work by inspiration rather than mimicry: I feel like MIA is onto something and want to know more about her, but don't quite identify with her image in any of her music videos

I know Scarface is a bad guy, but I'm sorry to see him die. Yet I don't care when his colleagues fall. I identify with the movie's sense of how the world turns. I have never adopted the perspective of Batman, but my understanding of his interests do preoccupy me. I can identify with a project (ending this senseless war), a person (the main character), a tone (dark sarcasm in Dr. Strangelove), or a style (gangster movies). Can I identify against something as well (the 'Jew Hunter' Hans Landa of *Inglourious Basterds*)?

Interpellated

Lovers and friends are usually quite meaningless details. In the family photo album.

'Who is that?'
    'Don't know, not family, though.'

What's it going to take before you take an interest in family? How long will it be before you learn to shut up and enjoy it, to love and be loved by your family? The family will be the truth of your life, the position from which you can understand your self that has grown up, aged, changed, and, in turn, taken up its self as an entrepreneurial project. You must return to the family and perhaps you will come to see its beauty. This you have many, many chances to come to understand.

There is a very different story that we tell about your place in the family.
    You were expected by the time you were born. You were inter-

pellated at birth, given a name that had already been decided in advance. Anticipated and expected. That is the origin.

It would be from this start that ideological subjectivization and its failure, or power and resistance, or systematicity and irregularity separate. And, at this exact same moment, that complex material relations, which you could chart as a dialectic, play out the hybridity by which the distinction wrought by a theory of interpellation diffuses.

Hybridity. Like how boysenberry bounces playfully as it recalls thorns all around it and you read it on the menu and it's in waffles and you wonder if they will be too expensive and then if they would be too sour. Connotations from childhood now associated strongly with family, significance from financial independence, a feeling from the stomach to the throat.

If there is childhood, stomach, and a budget for brunch, interpellation could be one more force in the overdetermination of every situation. Ok. But that there is an ongoing process of negotiating identity does suggest that interpellation as a theoretical mechanism establishes retroactive continuity by subsuming varying negotiations under the name of interpellation.

Name

To have your name replaced with a number, to have your identity recoded into something your parents did not choose for you, something unfamiliar, something suited for data processing by machines, surely it would destroy your very being.

What does your name mean? You first name, your middle name, your last name. There is a legal requirement that, for you to appear, there be a first and last name for you. Often, there's a limit to its length. It must be composed of roman letters, its capitalization may be lost or determined against your wishes, it cannot contain numbers. (There are actually many more legal rules for names, especially in some European countries.)

Names from India, transliterated for native English speakers, are often too long. Names from East Asia become unpronounceable and may be replaced, just to make life a little bit easier. Esther, Eunice, Sally.

The last name of many African-Americans comes from those who owned enslaved ancestors. Spanish naming customs become a confusing mess in the US paradigm.

Ellis Island renamed thousands of families after their country of origin, or for ethnic identity. The concept or image, by which one's child was to be addressed, disappears in the American system of formal names, which only identifies by strings of letters.

Names from most anywhere lose their pronunciation, they are 'butchered.' (To slaughter in an indiscriminate manner, not to carve meat into cuts.)

The stock of common American names has become boring and yet a kind of elementary privilege. Not a weird name, but a regular one: Lauren, Matt, Aaron, Joe, Leslie, Owen, Emily, and Charles. Yet the very nature of the arbitrary system by which we are primarily identified as individuals provides a means of variation. Change the spelling of the name: Britni, Izabella, Joshwa, Konner.

And yet, on a regular basis, many feel that their names identify them well, reflect where they come from and the choices of their family before them. That such a name is most appropriate, the best balance of a unique and truthful manner of addressing one another.

Empowerment Not Interpellation

Being recognized and named, perceived and identified with that perception, we are interpellated into power by the active force of our own identification. So what? Though we may be recognized as something (a citizen, a student, a customer), it is an open question how we will react to that label. Will you become the person they say you are? Will you resist? Or just forget about the whole thing?

We're much less interested in being known by a name than in getting what we want.

Empowerment has offered salvation for those frustrated with the identities by which they were perceived. Rape victims? No, rape survivors. Empowerment allows people to change their identity or work around an identity they know works against them. They would rather not be subject to a system of power where they lose out; they would rather be empowered. Well, who wouldn't?

Now nearly everyone wants to get empowered. When everyone wants something, capitalism (a purposing worker) gives a purpose to this desire: wanting empowerment can be turned into wanting stuff. Personal computers, advanced degrees, all-purpose drills, designer handbags, next generation mobile phones, luxury cars, Costco membership. These are powerful tools and symbols of power. They increase the capacities of an individual, making some things easier, making some dreams come true, changing the realities of their world.

Yet, in almost every case, this empowerment depends on a power sharing system where individuals get a tiny bit of a great big power (that is owned by someone else), and in so doing make that great big power more great and big and powerful. It takes millions of fans to make one superstar.

We support the great powers (Mac, Monsanto, Target, Lexus, Hennessy, Louis Vutton, Lady Gaga, Harry Potter, the US military, Facebook, Disney, Yum Foods) with our money and labor, with our word of mouth and enthusiasm, with our satisfaction and use of their services to do things in our own lives we could not do otherwise. We support them by accepting the empowerment they offer. (By fighting for the chance to take augment our selves with that power.)

Empowerment recruits support. But we don't think about it that way, because what I gain from using Google for search is immediate and obvious to me, while what they gain by my using their service is small, remote, and abstract. We can only see that we are better off empowered, not that we have therefore joined up with power.

The Hi-Tek Sector

Why do we still see technology as technical, when it is also social? Why do we define technologies as tools, when they are also our environment? If we still think of a thing as a technology, we see it as useful and confusing rather than cultural and traditional.

Myth of Inevitability

The problem with technological determinism is just like the problem with a bad sci-fi premise or the rantings of technofuturists. They act like, just because I am walking, and at this moment I'm headed North, I will soon arrive at the North Pole. Nothing will happen on the way, I will not turn before then. If I ever do arrive at the North Pole, they feel correct. The future is easy to see.

This is the same as the fallacy of the slippery slope. If we lose the right to talk on our cell phones in restaurants, fascism tomorrow.

The myth of inevitability is that because a technology exists and works (or would be cool if it did work), it will become ubiquitous and powerful. Kelly Gates argues that this myth makes us think facial recognition technology does work or will soon work despite all evidence to the contrary. What the fallacy misses is hard to make a general heuristic for properly avoiding. What it misses is a sufficient haziness to its logical organization. It is too logical, too true to its own rationality. In this way, it is also too forceful. Antonio Gramsci argues that hegemony (the organization/education of consent by the ruling party) works by claims of inevitability; myths of inevitability are employed as a tactic of hegemony.

The reason TV did not turn all brains to mush is that there are other things brains do than watch TV, and there are different things they do when watching TV. Outside factors do not remain outside forever, and, sadly, cannot be deduced from a rule.

Hackable Planet

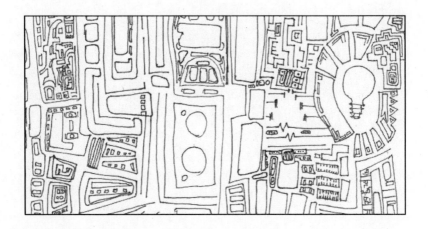

It's not that we really want to know who is going to hack the planet or why (Russian military outfits and Southeast Asian computer students, probably, but no one says it).

What is worrying and edgy and weird about hackers, as a phenomenon, is that so much of our society has been automated by computer systems that we have not yet learned to understand or trust it. Computers do our work, especially for the institutions that have lots of things to process or count. To the slave class of computers, the average hacker is a manipulative charlatan just trying to see how far he or she can get.

What is disconcerting is that ugly, young, whites from affluent families (who we all trusted had been well-contained by family, school, extra-curricular activities, preppy aspirations, benign artistic self-expression or countercultural hedonism) were messing with the systems everyone else had, for so many years, been learning to revere, while exploiting in their other ways.

Bill Gates embodies the cruel fact that nerds have money and power now because their tech-businesses have something powerful to offer the infrastructure of most everyone who is making music, math textbooks, mint candies, mineral processing facilities, major political decisions, measurements of an industry, or money hand over fist. When you, as a younger person than you are now, thought you did not want to be a nerd, maybe that was a mistake.

What is disconcerting is that these software systems, vulnerable to and ushered in by disgusting nerds (labeled and made disgusting by mass media, dating, corporate culture, and 'the arts'), are vulnerable technical systems that put a huge responsibility on the shoulders of a few civilized individuals who are probably themselves also nerds. We've learned to trust macho security teams and anal management types, but now the system is counting on weirdos.

As the decades have passed, hacking has come to mean viruses that are hard to distinguish from spam, glitches, pop-up ads, and the shit that Windows is actually programmed to do. Hackers now seem unimportant and the software doing all the boring work that can be automated easily has become a welcome part of our buggy society.

Content Neutral Data

To understand the information of the information age, first consider energy.

The standard physical measurements of *power* are measures of the rate at which *work* is performed or *energy* is used. Energy is the ability of a system to do work on other systems. The amount of energy in a jelly donut can lift a VW to the top of Mount Soledad.

Energy is uniform and can be generically put to use. All the forces (electromagnetic, gravitational, strong, and weak) partly express themselves in energy, work, and power.

This generic quality, however, is better at lifting masses over distance, running electric motors, and heating volumes of water than it is at giving me a nourishing breakfast, heating my poorly insulated room, or figuring out how to politely decline an invitation. Electricity is a privileged form of energy, alacrity in support staff is not. In fact, by the measure of energy, humans are not very efficient and most of their actions could be done with great savings by large gas turbines. If only a machine could be designed that would channel the energy properly.

This is the non-neutrality of energy: it is generic and uniform in a manner that undervalues, on principle, things we do value in practice.

Information is the same way. Information means data, which means a series of bits that are richer in information if they are harder to compress. Information theory privileges data that is readily interpretable. We register more information in a thing if it is explicit, if it is easy to extract, if we are prepared to take meaning from it. In everyday action, this means that textbooks, the plot of a movie, codes, lyrics, and mission statements are high in information. Yet, we know these texts can be very misleading.

Information is like energy, its generic and uniform sense of neutrality excludes and undervalues some of its cases. In this sense, we see more 'information' in the letters than in the font, in a billboard than in an underpass, in the nutritional information than in the food, in a brand name than in a shoe.

Upgrade

I want to get a better one.

Upgrades replace what came before. The thing I've got now is good; the upgrade will be better. The logic of the upgrade depends on a desire for more.

To accomplish this, there must exist criteria by which one thing can be definitively better than another. More memory, faster throughput, lower price, or a bigger screen.

The infinite particularity of one object must be ignored, for a moment, to allow a comparison by which one object is an upgrade for another. If you think about how the one TV reminds you of a great summer or has a really nice surface on top where you could balance a drink, it becomes hard to say whether this TV is better than the new, smaller, thinner, HD one. But if we are only counting number of pixels, contrast ratios, power consumption, and footprint in the living room, the new TV is better.

An upgrade is new, and new things have their own appeal.

Things that are old don't work perfectly, have idiosyncrasies, and are a bit worn. What this really means is that new consumer products have more recently been in controlled, standardized environments, so that if your phone has a problem when it's new, there is less range of what the problem might be than if the phone has been out of the factory, being used. It really means that we prefer upgrades because we don't know how to take responsibility for the way we use and maintain the things that we buy.

Typing

I generate words by pushing a single key for each letter of each word. The finger presses down a button that makes a tiny clicking sound and pops back up, letting me know that I've hit the key correctly. I can hit many keys per second. Maximum typing speeds on conventional keyboards are about 150 words per minute. When we type, we are almost never only typing. We are also using the mouse, monitor, and speakers. We may be using keyboard shortcuts or using the keyboard to give input other than text. Typing on a keyboard, in conjunction with heavy and fragile monitors and the mouse's need for a flat surface keep computer users sitting wrong. The posture of computer use would be a great thing to change, but we tend to accept it as the given cost for the privilege of using a computer.

One problem with typing is that the fingers misspell words that the mind 'knows' how to spell, and when you type faster you make more mistakes. Spell check (especially with autocorrect) can lessen the impact of this problem.

Spell check could be improved. A better spell check would look for errors between words, not just within a word. (Sot he word maybe spelled right, butt hat doesn't meant hat there I sno typo.) Second, it would learn a user's common mistakes and incorporate habitual misspellings (such as ot for to or eht for the into autocorrect). Third, spell check should question whether a word such as fro or pubic was used intentionally, and call the user's attention to these words that can be found in a dictionary but are probably not what the user intended. (Actually, you can do this last one now.)

We like typing. We could use speech recognition, or a chorded keyboard keyboard. But we don't. We have come to like the pace of typing. Or we like that, with typing, we can type in a flowing burst of words or in a stutter. With word processing, we can see what we are saying as written words. We feel more comfortable because we can see and control the final image of our ongoing actions. A favorite paint brush, an illusion of precision.

The hands typing become a second voice, one by which others will regard us and one that comes to feel like the sound of one's own thinking.

Know Your Tools

No, I don't know how the engine works of the car I drive at 35 in a 30 zone.

They say that we use technologies we don't even understand, which is a problem of modern times. Did the caveman, the original masculine generic of the tool-using human (i.e. the active subject), understand the stones so popular in the Stone Age?

Conchoidal fracture makes obsidian and flint easy to sharpen, because that's how the stone breaks. Other stones break in basically flat planes, but small conchoidal fractures can be added repeatedly to produce various shapes, and sharp edges in particular. Wikipedia still doesn't have a definite explanation of flint formation, which gives the stone its relevant properties. But this is how the stone breaks, and tools can, for whatever reason, be made with it.

No, we don't all understand the tools we use. Probably never have. A new question: Why is it sometimes suggested that we should?

Comparing and Connecting

Making a connection is an action. Comparisons do not just suggest themselves, someone acts on the suggestion. Our procedures of discrimination allow us to sort things out and respond to them appropriately, but sometimes we do a pretty bad job of it.

Differences | Different Ones

Difference is a relational condition. Difference is between or among, a unit of distinction. This is the difference of biodiversity and affirmative action. Differentiation subdivides what is known, classifies by categories, territorializes by strata, or appends to geometries of connection.

Biodiversity holds in relation necessary minima and maxima for environmental variables: at least this many black footed ferrets, no more than that many lionfish in the Atlantic. Likewise, affirmative action's interest in reproducing demographic proportions of a population's variation in an institution's personnel treats variation along given lines (e.g. race and sex, understood by definitions selected to limit liability). Not an indictment of affirmative action.

Where might we put the taste of sugar that invents sweetness, the look of an animal from which we learn hazy caution, the variety and depth of our experience of beer or wine? To call it prior to semiotization would be banishment, and to understand it as parallel-to or networked-in understates the inequality of their powers.

Differents are different things beside the semiotization by which their differences become clear or systematic. Mr. Ed the Horse, pineapple colored interior paint, pain, the gleam of utility, this, vanilla flavor, pages that are difficult to turn, jk3nssD, fixing the tongue of my boots. Are these different things unable to remain different when listed together; is a sequence of terms with commas already units with distinctions?

The terms of difference enthusiastically assimilate what is different, turning pain into one of a range of feelings and Mr. Ed into a talking animal. What is different becomes, *through the act of comparison*, a case with a difference. Sometimes the translation goes the other way, from differences to something altogether different.

Utopian vision starts from differences (no more racism, no deaths from malnourishment, a positive concept of peace) and arrives at an absolutely *different* ideal: city in the clouds, casitas in the woods, a world of nanotechnology. The lesbian island city would not have heteropatriarchy, and we won't worry about its immigration policies or treatment of closeted heterosexuals. Let's not get too specific, after all the demand for immediate alternatives when you offer criticism forces us to return to the problematic that we're trying to work around.

This effect, the absolute vision of difference we end up with is, in its vagueness, immune to comparisons by which it would revert to relative differences.

Discrimination Machine

It is not coherent, unified, regular, or functioning quite according to plan. It is a machine. It is doing the job, because it is doing a job and that is getting something done which we will say was the job we should have expected anyway.

Discrimination takes place by processes. Comments in the street. Responses to your voice on the phone. Laws controlling rights and privileges by home address. Hiring children of friends. Making police officers want to let you off this time.

A discrimination machine filters, by mechanisms, sorting out what might continue and what would be redirected.

A suit is not just a costume. It's a costume kept alive specifically for its power as a discrimination machine: who can get the best one with the nicest details and, above all, the best tailoring. What does best mean? Are you up to date, sufficiently traditional, overly French, generally respectable, comfortable, careful with money? Exactly questions the machinery offers as opportunities to distinguish your good taste.

Natural selection is another such machine. The effects of discrimination depend of course on sorting. What is selected for and against? The discrimination machine does not do all the work here, there must be forces that align behind the different directions contents can travel. Reproduction, population, heritability, death.

We don't just say that species with greater reproductive success are more fit. It isn't really important if people speak of fitness as good or bad. The problem appears here as the force of life that keeps the living together as life on earth. In a catalog of all species that ever were, fitness doesn't matter. In that happy underworld where the dead collect, fitness is a curse extending bit by bit the suffering of life on your children and children's children.

Moralizing about evolution, or even taking pride in having been selected, is, in this way, to confirm the processes of discrimination. Insofar as you're proud to have made it while others fell, the machinery of discrimination chose well.

Yet, some people are very proud to be survivors. To have been sorted into life, while others, for a great variety of reasons, were not.

Universal Relativism

I use the past tense here as retconning rather than studying history. It establishes retroactive continuity, where none before existed, as has become common in comics and TV shows. A new history of the past appears and we act as if it were there the whole time. Retcon allow us to ask the question 'what history here today has the force of having occurred as the past?' instead of simply asking 'what are the historical facts?'

Relativism has emerged as the scapegoat for the problems of the universalism it once tried to oppose (solve the problems of). Everyone is not striving for economic growth, we are all striving for our own culturally specific ideals. Because, in order to be universalistic about any rules, it was necessary to make exception and qualifications to the extent that things no longer looked, at a glance, in any particular instance, to be universal, everything seemed relative. But it was always only relative to other things, and usually this was not a boundless rhizome of relatives (a social network), but something much more like a family tree. These are all 2nd generation children. Versus, these are all Mike's Facebook friends.

As it happens, cultures are not isometric. A chief is not the same thing as a president, a lassi is not the same as a milkshake. However, in order to manage global market penetration, there had to be some kind of category of product that Coca-Cola would be introduced as a rival to, or substitute for. 'Thandi means Coca-Cola!' It is not because relativism is so bright and true, it's because this kind of move puts a limit to Western appropriation and demolition of differences, at different sites both theoretical and practical. Really, this kind of passive tolerance called respect for difference mixed with occasional contemplation is quite affected and not much of a step from orientalist fantasy and an educated tradition of racism. But the new ambiguity was going to make us cautious.

The result is that the basis for societies' similarities was not Bangladesh, but a kind of (vague, abstract, carefully guarded and deliberately arcane) Western theorization of human cultures. And this does not mean Europe. Contemporary Germany, it turns out, is just as susceptible to relativist abduction as any other site of fieldwork. This abduction let everyone be in some way equivalent, instead of inferior. But it also forces us to account for who that everyone might be and what kind of thing they ('we') are all equal to. Cleverly, 'Western' feminists understood the limits of cultural relativism as part of a liberal/progressive agenda, and have been pretty bold in cutting the crap when it doesn't help them, and judging some cultural practices in universal terms other than the universal differences and respect due to other forms of human life.

We = Multiplicity of I

Not we, the people. Imagine instead a we that does not refer to a community I am a person speaking in. A we who is how hard it is to get a grasp of what it would have been to know what me this I is. A we that is what makes I never final. A we of everyone I could have been, of every kind of person I've seen myself for a second as, but been unable to hold onto that horror of. A we that strains to include every perspective I have once been close to, been exposed to, taken seriously.

From this we the I can change. Not I, the grammar of a first person singular subject. Not I, the avatar of me. That me is a different effect of writing that helps find itself through reading, a figure in the process of a reader reading something autobiographical (generative of an author from the writing). I as the instance of a we which is a non-uniform field of possibilities.

This multiplicity of the first person allows creative exploration representing not concrete individuals, who we will always strain to represent properly, but the rogue material that cannot be reduced to the simplification of experience that is widely known as the self.

Opposite of this: The Individual 11. An individualist group who share the same views so completely they don't even have to talk. Yet a group of identical actors playing out the program of a mind-control infection. The self-actualized, subject without anxiety, still fresh from the mint, and insistent on its own self-identity with its will. The person you would be if you could really Do What You Like & Like What You Do. Only violently individualist.

Learning Racism

How do we learn about race? How do we learn not to point at someone who is pale, whose eyes are narrow, or whose skin gets ashy? How do we learn to understand and respect differences, and how do we learn what these differences are? We have to learn both racism and racial tolerance, which are not distinct topics.

Asian-Americans often live in relation to the common impression that they all want to be doctors, know kung fu, are good with numbers, or have a special connection to laundry. To understand Indian people it would help to know something about what is commonly called their traditional family structure and gender roles.

When you learn that most Chinese people have straight, black hair most of the time, you've learned a stereotype and begun to learn how to be sensitive about the whole hair thing. When you learn not to insult white people openly for their careless disrespect (but indefatigable curiosity) for other languages and cultures, you've learned how to do your part in the continuation of racism.

The two tend to overlap. But one can learn racism without learning how to be nice about it. The reverse, however, is not really possible.

Interconnection

'Everything is connected.' No.

Interconnection is wrong because not everything is connected, not everything is connective, and we cannot recognize or understand most connections.

    The interconnection thesis states that everything is connected, lines connect things in network diagrams, that make everything within a system relative to everything else (a local deployment of universal relativism). These relations are over-normalized (having an organ is 'a relation' just like the relation of having a crush or having a drink). They reduce encounters to lines of relation (dogs meet at the park the same as phone and charger or cars that collide on the highway). These summary relations of interconnection treat very different situations as examples of a basically singular system that arrogantly presumes to be universal, but is actually still quite particular (lines and flows are specific models from geometry and engineering). The approach presumes all things are connective, yet most of the ground is dirt and not roots.

There is another issue with interconnection: the combination of what we don't know with which direction we can imagine causal effects going. We assume that the one-way causal links we do know about (runoff flowing downstream) are the whole story.

Tracing pollution back to its source shows that there are connections we don't understand and cannot foresee. So the lesson is to worry about polluting generally (any pollution, anywhere), to worry about how what is done here impacts generally what happens there. Having found a connection (traced back pollution), the interconnection thesis warns that we should be wary of this particular link. Conservative environmentalism. The delicate food web.

Isn't it also true that unexpected relations prove we will not know how things relate before they actually meet one another? Isn't it also true that complex and unforeseeable movements can make the world resilient and not just delicate?

Because we can only really point to connections that have been proven, or are plausible, interconnection mistakes relations with which we are familiar for relations by which the world proceeds. Resilience comes from dynamics that persist against other ones, from strength that arises out of destruction, from relations that had not before expressed themselves (real secrets).

When it becomes a systematic principle, a universalizing ideological claim about 'everything,' it ignores numbness, resilience, and the potential of what exists now to yield unexpected futures.

Pathways

Sometimes they want to build paths that follow the routes people actually walk. Then the walking that we do anyway will happen on their paths: slightly faster, without damage to surrounding landscaping, appearing as if our behavior and their design match.

Sometimes they want to build walkways for other reasons, as part of a pretty design: pathways that encircle spaces, mark a perimeter, connect paved areas, cut the lawn into four equal pieces, permit wheel-chair access. Then we make our own shortcuts, we walk on the grass, cut corners, step on flowers.

What the pathway always does, though, is suggest (advise) a path along the basic routes people actually walk, in the general direction of pedestrians coming from one point and going to another. The pathway negotiates your walking onto its specialized surface.

A walkway does not just offer a route, as do boulders strewn along the slope of a mountain, but displays a design that inspires in us a confidence: we might fit into this plan. It is not just a matter of our convenience, we do not walk through rubble, wilderness, or enemy territory. There is an institution, an owner, people who maintain the grounds, architecture prepared into which our entrance has been anticipated. Will we be best served by the design? This is the point at which walking along walkways depends upon trust, effects a quotidian loyalty, or is a tactic of your own life.

Works Drawn On and Recommended

Baudrillard, Jean. 1994. *Simulacra and Simulation*. Ann Arbor: University of Michigan Press.

Blade: Trinity. 2004. David Goyer. New Line Cinema.

Bolter, Jay David, and Richard Grusin. 2000. *Remediation: Understanding New Media*. The MIT Press.

Brown, Wendy. 2001. *Politics Out of History*. Princteon: Princeton University Press.

Chaloupka, William. 1992. *Knowing Nukes: the Politics and Culture of the Atom*. Minneapolis: University of Minnesota Press.

Chaloupka, William. 1999. *Everybody Knows: Cynicism in America*. Minneapolis: University of Minnesota Press.

Chameleon Street. 1989. Wendell B. Harris Jr. Gathsemane 84.

Charlie and the Chocolate Factory. 2005. Tim Burton. Warner Bros.

Danger Mouse. *The Grey Album*. 2004.

Dean, Jodi.2005-2007. *iCite*. http://jdeanicite.typepad.com/

Deleuze, Gilles, and Felix Guattari. 1987. A Thousand Plateaus: Capitalism and Schizophrenia. Trans. Brian Massumi. Minneapolis: Univ. of Minnesota Press.

Deleuze, Gilles, and Felix Guattari. 1994. 'Percept, Affect, Concept.' In *What Is Philosophy?* New York: Columbia University Press.

Donnie Darko. 2001. Richard Kelly. Pandora Cinema.

Dr. Strangelove or: How I Learned to Stop Worrying and Love the Bomb. 1964. Stanley Kubrick. Columbia Pictures.

Stargate. 1994. Roland Emmerich. Canal+.

Foucault, Michel. 1977. *Discipline and Punish: The Birth of the Prison*.New York: Pantheon Books.

Foucault, Michel. 1990. *The History of Sexuality, Vol. 1: An Introduction*. New York: Vintage.

Gates, Kelly. 2011. *Our Biometric Future: Facial Recognition Technology and the Culture of Surveillance*. New York: New York

University Press.

Ghost in the Shell: Solid State Society. 2006. Kenji Kamiyama. Kôkaku Kidôtai Seisaku Iinkai and Production I.G.

Golumbia, David. 2009. *The Cultural Logic of Computation*. Cambridge Mass.: Harvard University Press.

Gramsci, Antonio. 1972. *Selections from the Prison Notebooks of Antonio Gramsci*. New York: International Publishers.

Groundhog Day. 1993. Harold Ramis. Columbia Pictures.

Inglourious Basterds. 2009. Quentin Tarantino. Weinstein and Universal Pictures.

Lingis, Alphonso. 2000. *Dangerous Emotions*. Berkeley: University of California Press.

May, Jon, and Nigel Thrift. 2001. *TimeSpace: Geographies of Temporality*. New York: Routledge.

McGee, Kyle. 2010. 'Machining Fantasy: Spinoza, Hume, and the Miracle in a Politics of Desire.' *Philosophy & Social Criticism* 36 (September): 837–856.

Mearls, Mike. 2008. *Monster Manual*. Renton Wash.: Wizards of the Coast.

Odier, Daniel. 1970. *The Job: Interviews with William S. Burroughs*. New York: Grove Press.

Scarface. 1983. Brian De Palma. Universal Pictures.

Schlag, Pierre. 1997. 'Law as the Continuation of God by Other Means.' *California Law Review* 85: 427–440.

Shaviro, Steven. 1997. *Doom Patrols: A Theoretical Fiction About Postmodernism*. New York: Serpent's Tail.

Shaviro, Steven. 2009. *Without Criteria: Kant, Whitehead, Deleuze, and Aesthetics*. Cambridge Mass.: MIT Press.

Simmel, Georg. 1971. *On Individuality and Social Forms: Selected Writings*. Ed. Donald Nathan Levine. Chicago: University of Chicago Press.

Sukiyaki Western Django. 2007. Miike Takashi. Sony Pictures Entertainment.

The Dark Knight. 2008. Christopher Nolan. Warner Bros.

The Postman. 1997 Kevin Costner. Tig Productions and Warner
Bros.

Contemporary culture has eliminated both the concept of the public and the figure of the intellectual. Former public spaces – both physical and cultural – are now either derelict or colonized by advertising. A cretinous anti-intellectualism presides, cheerled by expensively educated hacks in the pay of multinational corporations who reassure their bored readers that there is no need to rouse themselves from their interpassive stupor. The informal censorship internalized and propagated by the cultural workers of late capitalism generates a banal conformity that the propaganda chiefs of Stalinism could only ever have dreamt of imposing. Zer0 Books knows that another kind of discourse – intellectual without being academic, popular without being populist – is not only possible: it is already flourishing, in the regions beyond the striplit malls of so-called mass media and the neurotically bureaucratic halls of the academy. Zer0 is committed to the idea of publishing as a making public of the intellectual. It is convinced that in the unthinking, blandly consensual culture in which we live, critical and engaged theoretical reflection is more important than ever before.